Improving the Context for Inclusio...

This timely book addresses the need for increasing multi-agency capacity in schools, as the success of initiatives such as Every Child Matters or 'personalised learning' depends on teachers understanding the challenges faced by young people in learning effectively and happily in their school.

The authors of this thought-provoking book present and analyse case studies of collaborative action research, illustrating what is needed in practice for teachers to engage with inclusion for the benefit of their pupils and themselves. The essential elements of success with inclusion are revealed, including:

- the importance of identifying issues that teachers see as relevant;
- how teachers can achieve meaningful collaboration in addressing the issues;
- the necessity of paying careful attention to the consequences of the changes that they make;
- incorporating practical considerations such as critical support from outsiders;
- the role of facilitators such as educational psychologists in working with groups of teachers to support their development through action research;
- how to facilitate change through making use of resources that are already available in the education system.

Improving the Context for Inclusion is fascinating reading for all students of education, especially those with an interest in inclusion. Teachers, school leaders and those working in education services will gain an invaluable insight into how to create an inclusive school environment by personalising the development of teachers.

Andy Howes is a Senior Lecturer in the School of Education at the University of Manchester.

S.M.B. Davies is a Senior Lecturer in the School of Education Studies and Social Inclusion at Trinity College Carmarthen, University of Wales.

Sam Fox is a Lecturer in Education at Edge Hill University.

Improving Learning TLRP

Series Editor: Andrew Pollard, Director of the ESRC Teaching and Learning Programme

Improving Learning, Skills and Inclusion: the impact of policy on
post-compulsory education
Frank Coffield, Sheila Edward, Ian Finlay, Ann Hodgson,
Ken Spours and Richard Steer

Improving Classroom Learning with ICT
Rosamund Sutherland, Susan Robertson and Peter John

Improving Inter-professional Collaborations: multi-agency
working for children's wellbeing
Anne Edwards, Harry Daniels, Tony Gallagher, Jane Leadbetter
and Paul Warmington

Improving Learning in College: rethinking literacies across the
curriculum (forthcoming)
Roz Ivanic, Richard Edwards, David Barton, Zoe Fowler,
Gregg Mannion, Kate Miller and Marilyn Martin-Jones

Improving Learning in Later Life (forthcoming)
Alexandra Withnall

Improving Mathematics at Work: the need for
techno-mathematical literacies (forthcoming)
Celia Hoyles, Richard Noss, Phillip Kent and Arthur Bakker

Improving Research through User Engagement (forthcoming)
Mark Rickinson, Anne Edwards and Judy Sebba

Improving What is Learned at University: an exploration of the
social and organisational diversity of university education
(forthcoming)
John Brennan

Improving the Context for Inclusion

Personalising teacher development through collaborative action research

Andy Howes, S.M.B. Davies and Sam Fox

Routledge
Taylor & Francis Group

LONDON AND NEW YORK

First published 2009
by Routledge
2 Park Square, Milton Park, Abingdon, Oxon OX14 4RN

Simultaneously published in the USA and Canada
by Routledge
270 Madison Ave, New York, NY 10016

Routledge is an imprint of the Taylor & Francis Group, an informa business

© 2009 Andy Howes, S.M.B. Davies and Sam Fox

Typeset in Stone Sans and Charter ITC
by Keystroke, 28 High Street, Tettenhall, Wolverhampton
Printed and bound in Great Britain
by TJ International Ltd, Padstow, Cornwall

British Library Cataloguing in Publication Data
A catalogue record for this book is available from the British Library

Library of Congress Cataloging in Publication Data
Howes, Andy.
  Improving the context for inclusion : personalising teacher
  development through collaborative action research / Andy Howes,
  Sam Fox and Sue Davies.
      p. cm.
    Includes bibliographical references and index.
  1. Inclusive education—Great Britain. 2. School improvement
  programs—Great Britain. 3. Action research in education—Great
  Britain. 4. Teachers—In-service training—Great Britain. I. Fox, Sam.
  II. Davies, Sue. III. Title. IV. Title: Personalising teacher development
  through collaborative action research.
  LC1203.G7H69 2009
  371.9′0460941—dc22   2009000262

ISBN10: 0–415–47341–1 (hbk)
ISBN10: 0–415–47342–X (pbk)
ISBN10: 0–203–87513–3 (ebk)

ISBN13: 978–0–415–47341–5 (hbk)
ISBN13: 978–0–415–47342–2 (pbk)
ISBN13: 978–0–203–87513–1 (ebk)

Contents

Series editor's preface

The *Improving Learning* series showcases findings from projects within ESRC's Teaching and Learning Research Programme (TLRP) – the UK's largest ever coordinated educational research initiative.

Books in the *Improving Learning* series are explicitly designed to support 'evidence-informed' decisions in educational practice and policy-making. In particular, they combine rigorous social and educational science with high awareness of the significance of the issues being researched.

Working closely with practitioners, organisations and agencies covering all educational sectors, the Programme has supported many of the UK's best researchers to work on the direct improvement of policy and practice to support learning. Over sixty projects have been supported, covering many issues across the life course. We are proud to present the results of this work through books in the *Improving Learning* series.

Each book provides a concise, accessible and definitive *overview* of innovative findings from a TLRP investment. If more advanced information is required, the books may be used as a gateway to academic journals, monographs, websites, etc. On the other hand, shorter summaries and *Research Briefings* on key findings are also available via the Programme's website at www.tlrp.org.

We hope that you will find the analysis and findings presented in this book are helpful to you in your work on improving outcomes for learners.

Andrew Pollard
Director, TLRP
Institute of Education, University of London

Acknowledgements

This is a book about making sense of practice, and about learning through the attempt to develop more inclusive practice. Many people have contributed to this learning process and not all of them can be mentioned by name here.

Teacher action research is dependent on the engagement of teachers, and research on this process depends on the willingness of those teachers to go further in facilitating and assisting with the generation of data, and the presence of research staff in classrooms and staffrooms. We are grateful to all the teachers and headteachers who agreed to take part in Prosiect Dysgu Cydradd.

Particular thanks go to the six educational psychologists who were part of the core research team and without whose generous participation and wholehearted engagement neither the development in schools, nor the research project around it would have been possible: Adele Christopher, Mark Hancock, Bethan Roberts, Gill Rhydderch, Gary Squires and Anwen Thomas. We wish to thank the members of our advisory group for their stimulating and encouraging feedback as the project developed. Four university colleagues in particular, Peter Farrell, Sian Swann, Heddwen Davies and Tim Carroll, played a crucial role in the project but are not listed in the authorship of this book.

Thanks are also due to the Teaching and Learning Research Programme office, especially Mary James as our critical friend, and to the administrative staff for their efficient and friendly assistance throughout the project. In Trinity College, translation services were invaluable in dealing with transcripts of interviews, project briefings and materials. In both Trinity College and the University of Manchester, our thanks go to administrative staff who dealt efficiently with the finances for the project, and for the organisation associated with dissemination workshops in Swansea and Manchester.

Part I

What are the issues?

Chapter 1

Inclusion is a challenge

This chapter explains inclusion in schools as an inherently educational aspiration. A range of discourses and approaches to educational inclusion are introduced and referenced, along with a group of interventions which focus on actions outside schools which aim (among other things) to support access and participation in education. Then the focus shifts to teachers. The challenge that inclusion presents for teachers is explored, with an argument for focusing on the particular context of secondary schools. The chapter ends by arguing that teachers are so influential in schools that inclusion can only be addressed with their active engagement.

The starting point of this book is in an understanding of inclusion as a particular challenge in secondary schools, and as an issue on which schools can move forward only with the engagement of teaching staff. In this chapter we consider the complex discourse around inclusion, and relate it to some significant contemporary policy developments, including Every Child Matters and personalised learning, and also to educational agendas like pupil voice.

This is a hopeful book, in that it presents an approach to developing a more inclusive education system which depends on the professional engagement of teachers, but it is not a naively hopeful book (Grace 1994, pp. 19–20; Thrupp and Tomlinson 2005). We recognise all too clearly that meaningful inclusion represents a particularly challenging aim in secondary schools. There are many secondary school pupils who see much of their schooling as irrelevant, and feel themselves to be inadequate at school; and many secondary school teachers who recognise and are dissatisfied with this situation but find it difficult to alter. What is missing in many schools is a process by which teachers can begin to alter the status quo. This book aims to identify and explore one such process.

The concept of inclusion as used in this book involves those who work in education posing questions about the way schools (and subjects, and lessons) are organised in relation to the engagement of young people in the educational process, and then taking action to address this issue. This includes:

- asking questions about how schools adapt to and work effectively with the diversity of their student populations;
- finding out about and working with what pupils bring with them to school rather than viewing differences in terms of deficits;
- taking greater account of the understandings that young people have of school and education, rather than seeking only to engage more young people in existing school practice.

Educational inclusion, then, involves treating each person as a human being, whether pupils, teachers, support staff or managers. Many young people in school come to be perceived and treated as if they occupied a single dimension, for example, as failed students, having ADHD, as trouble-makers, or as compliant and interested learners. Teachers can lose the sensitivity they need to see and interact with children and young people in their contemporary and social location, and with their expectations, constraints, hopes and fears. For us, educational inclusion incorporates a **view of the human self** that finds meaning in relationship to others, rather than being about the development of isolated individuals, and a **view of education** as an open-ended process of becoming for each person, rather than the achievement of pre-specified ends; it has a moral purpose, concerned with preparing each person to live a good life; and it is located in a particular historical and social context. This perspective draws on Fielding's (2006) presentation of the philosopher John MacMurray in his consideration of the institutional life of schools in terms of human rather than functional purpose. Conceived of in this way, inclusion can never result from a quick bolt-on solution to a pressing problem. Instead, the knowledge and understanding on which inclusion is necessarily based can only be gained through ongoing dialogue involving teachers and learners in the institution that they inhabit together. Inclusion, in other words, can be sustained and developed only when there are processes in place through which solutions to problems and issues can emerge, and where these solutions primarily involve change and adaptation in the cultures, rules and practices of the school and classroom, and change only secondarily in the individuals and groups who appear not to fit in.

Inclusion in this sense is a challenge for teachers and for those who lead and manage schools. Of course many teachers consistently develop and organise effective and inclusive lessons, for example, through the use of images, games, and assessment for learning techniques to facilitate response to the difficulties, or surprising capabilities that they identify among their pupils. But this is not the whole story. Over recent years in England and Wales, many teachers have become used to receiving directives, and tend to express frustration when invited instead to spend time using their own experience and understanding to explore ways forward. Indeed, one of the stimuli behind the project on which this book is based was a seminar on inclusion and action research at Trinity College Carmarthen in 2004, in which the teachers attending expressed disappointment at not being given directions for how to develop their practice. Many teachers feel constantly short of time, and cannot necessarily see the value of engaging in questions of practice with each other as peers. Yet educational inclusion as we understand it requires a community of practitioners engaged primarily in learning with and from each other, with an open-ended agenda for development rather than a predetermined list of competencies to tick off, or the latest educational fad to accomplish. We see the need to counter those dominant discourses around schooling which reduce teachers to individual technicians in a system designed and run elsewhere. We need to know how to create a context in schools in which dialogue and understanding between teachers and learners is valued, in which teachers see themselves as professional learners, and where they recognise the primacy of their own expertise in responding to the young people they are teaching, rather than the promise of the latest initiative.

In this book, we aim to justify our belief in a process which can help to construct such a context, in which developments towards inclusion can be explored, supported and understood within and beyond the school community. Such a process requires a degree of clarity in respect of inclusion in practice (this chapter); the valuing of particular features of teacher professional development (Chapter 2), and a critical, reflective approach towards change within the school and its communities (Chapters 3–6). The book concludes by considering what we learn from all this about improving the context for inclusion in schools.

In the following sections of this chapter, we first consider the various discourses of inclusion and explain our particular focus on the engagement of young people in learning. We then look at broader interventions around school and community, and explore the limitations of their impact on teachers' practice. The implications for teachers of our approach to inclusion are then explored, with particular reference to the challenges faced by teachers in secondary schools.

Discourses of inclusion

Inclusion, like 'reflection' (Morrison 1996, p. 317), has become a portmanteau term, used for such a variety of purposes that it has passed beyond ambiguity and is becoming a source of confusion. As a further complication, different definitions of inclusion dominate in different countries. It may be that the use of the word 'inclusion' in the title of this book is misleading to some readers, although we hope to show that similar issues underlie many different approaches to inclusion, and that therefore there is value in our approach to people working in many different contexts. In any case, the widespread application of the term 'inclusion' demands that it still be addressed, and so it is helpful to briefly review some of the main uses to which it is put. To do this, we begin with a 'typology of six ways of ways of thinking about inclusion' (Ainscow *et al.* 2006, p. 15). In an analysis that builds on one by Clough (2000, p. 8), these authors show how inclusion has been considered in many, sometimes contradictory ways over the past few decades, and how those approaches continue to influence practice, with complex and sometimes perverse consequences. They discuss:

- Inclusion as a concern with disabled students and others categorised as 'having special educational needs'.
- Inclusion as a response to disciplinary exclusion.
- Inclusion in relation to all groups seen as being vulnerable to exclusion.
- Inclusion as 'Education for All'.
- Inclusion as developing the school for all.
- Inclusion as a principled approach to education and society.

(Ainscow *et al.* 2006, p. 15)

Defining inclusion in any of these ways has consequences for the types of activities and the ways of knowing that will be seen to promote inclusion. Each of these definitions of inclusion has merit, but they also create obstacles in the way they are deployed in practice. The first three definitions spring from the best of intentions in a need to address a perceived injustice, and to overcome the barriers to education for particular pupils. Thus, for example, the inclusion of disabled students and those seen as having special educational needs into mainstream schools is a (qualified) legal requirement in the United States, and to a lesser extent in many other countries including England and Wales, and 'inclusion' is widely taken to signify this focus. Inclusion is also widely understood as the converse of exclusion from school (as a result of challenging behaviour, for example); and school inspection in England and Wales has extended this notion to be a concern for all groups vulnerable to exclusion. Each of these can be justified in terms of practical necessity for all young people concerned.

However, the practice that follows these definitions also creates new problems, because they so easily lead back to a limiting of educational opportunity, based more or less on the identification and indeed extension of differences between people, and on their 'constitutional' characteristics (Thomas and Loxley 2007, p. 141). There is a critical sense in the listing of vulnerable groups 'that there may be some common processes which link the different forms of exclusion experienced by, say, children with disabilities, children who are excluded from their schools for disciplinary reasons and people living in poor communities' (Ainscow et al. 2006, pp. 19–20). In practice however, the invitation to analyse and interrogate the origins of such processes goes unnoticed, and the listing of groups becomes yet another way to categorise and label pupils.

In countries of the Global South, inclusion often has yet another meaning – it is widely linked to the aim of Education for All, and concerns mainly the issue of increasing enrolments in schools in the context of poverty and lack of access. Somewhat similar to this is the aim of developing the school for all, to establish a properly comprehensive system in which school development is about reducing barriers to learning and participation for all pupils. This is the basis, for example, of the widely referenced Index for Inclusion (Booth et al. 2000). Both of these approaches avoid any categorisation of groups, but in practice have been easily subverted or subordinated to other agendas because they lack any specific focus or sense of challenge – they are hard to argue against in general, but they provide relatively little direction with which to pursue particular issues.

As a consequence, Ainscow et al. (2006) argue for an approach based on values and principles as the most robust, perhaps incorruptible way of moving towards such a state of inclusion. They link this to the UNESCO (2001) formulation of inclusion as a 'reform that supports and welcomes diversity amongst all learners' (Ainscow *et al.* 2006, p. 2), and characterise the approach as *'school improvement with attitude'* (p. 1). An explicit approach to values helps to avoid the dangers that 'deflect attention away from the deeply unjust nature of the world' (Fielding 2006, p. 363), dangers which are certainly present in the discourses of inclusion as school development, where much talk about inclusion can appear to be cosy, based on a romanticised view of the human person who floats, as it were, detached from economic context, with no biography and subject to no social expectations or constraints.

The values approach is one that assumes relatively little about educational settings in general, and approaches inclusion as a process of developing practice in a specific context according to a set of inclusive and educational values and principles. Certainly it embraces some general features of inclusive practice: some practices are

> so integral to our conception of inclusion that they define themselves: for example the reduction of bullying among children and adults in education or the building of relationships of collaboration and respect, or the involvement in schools of parents/carers and their surrounding communities.
>
> (Ainscow *et al.* 2006, p. 26)

In other words, some aspects of schools are too obviously excluding to ignore. In general however, inclusion means believing in and working out the consequences of a commitment to equality of opportunity, for example. 'Given our focus on values, rather than on practices and forms of provision, inclusion, we thought, could only be defined as the embodiment of those values *in particular contexts*' (Ainscow *et al.* 2006, p. 26).

In this approach, then, there is little certainty as to the practices which might best embody inclusive principles and values. As a consequence, a gap often opens up between the values rhetoric and the development of practice, with practitioners bearing nearly all the responsibility to work out the implications in their own contexts, and only partially engaging in this process. As a practical strategy for discerning and developing a manageable focus for change in those contexts, this is problematic. The discourse of values is not well linked to discourses of teaching and learning, and so it is hard to work out the implications of inclusive values for the teacher's role. Which, for example, is the value that foregrounds the quality of teachers' relationships with children and young people? What values justify and promote an educational dialogue between teachers and relatively marginalised pupils, or coordination and practical understanding with other local policies such as housing and social services? How in practice should teachers investigate the underpinnings of their pedagogy, looking for processes which encourage comparison between pupils and widen the differences between them?

We have found it helpful to bear in mind a more particular view of what the inclusive school would be like. Going beyond our original definition of inclusion as incorporating a specific view of the human person, and a corresponding view of education, Fielding (2006) has proposed the following characteristics of what he describes as an intentional, emergent person-centred school:

> [T]he person-centred learning community is guided by its commitment to the functional arrangements and interactions of the school being firmly committed to wider human purposes. . . . The organizational architecture of the school is heavily influenced by the acknowledged values and aspirations that express its distinctive character. Wide-ranging formal and informal arrangements amongst staff and between students and staff ensure many voices are heard and engaged. Pastoral and academic arrangements relate to each other synergistically with the needs of young people as persons providing the touchstone of aspiration and the arbiter of difficulty or conflict of interest. CPD [continuing professional development] is wide ranging in both its processes and its substance. Often collegial, occasionally communal, it is enquiry driven and learning oriented, e.g. encouraging hermeneutic or critical approaches to action research.
>
> (Fielding 2006, p. 360)

This is not a development programme, although it does contain some indications of developmental structures and processes, and we see it as a dynamic and challenging pen-portrait of features of a school that is taking inclusion seriously as a fundamental value. In a similar way, we see much of the discourse of inclusion as speaking of an intention to influence schools in a radical direction, but often lacking a programme for action. Other attempts to offer an approach to changing the system are much more direct. Hopkins (2007), for example, argues for 'system leadership' in education as the most effective way of contributing to the development of a more equal and just society. The central systems idea is that there are many aspects which must be addressed at the same time to improve schools, and Hopkins provides an outline of the implications for leadership to bring that about. He articulates his values in passing, promoting an approach to personalised learning that reflects the 'moral purpose of education', urging a consistent focus by teachers on *matching* 'what is taught and how it is taught to the individual learner as a person' (p. 52). He argues too for a particular approach to professionalised teaching, involving coaching and mentoring, along with a framework of accountability and energetic networking, as interrelated and necessary drivers in bringing about a system comprising more uniformly good schools. From a national policy perspective, all this may well add up to a beguiling and integrating picture. However, what Hopkins consistently underplays are the learning processes through which teachers make sense of their practice. In Hopkins' system, professionalisation corresponds to a precise positioning of teachers in relation to policy; teachers are required to define themselves and their practice according to a particular framework. This is disempowering for teachers, and empowering for those who construct the framework. It does little to accommodate the diversity of teachers and their classroom practices, or teachers' diverse experiences of learning and development. It disregards teachers' diverse ways of knowing and being. This is a theme that will be developed in Chapter 2.

These three approaches (school improvement with attitude, the person-centred learning community and systems leadership) are based on very different assumptions about the knowing and learning of teachers, about which more will be said in the next chapter. We propose another approach, related to that of Ainscow *et al.* and Fielding, but constructed in a way that we hope will lead teachers more effectively towards implications for practice. In our understanding, although educational inclusion is best seen embodying a particular moral view of the human person and of education, and therefore a particular set of connected values and principles, it does not necessarily follow that the best way to develop inclusion is to start by thinking and reflecting on those values and trying to come up with useful responses or adjustments to practice. As we have seen, such an approach is extremely demanding for practitioners, because it suggests so many potential areas for action; besides which, the interaction of different values in a particular context means that determining the right course of action is problematic. In any case, if inclusion does comprise a connected set of values, then a group of teachers starting from a meaningful practical issue are likely to find themselves discussing these values as they grapple with the issues raised.

One solution to these difficulties regarding starting points is to approach the broader issues of inclusion by way of an initially relatively narrow focus. In our project, we decided to invite teachers to focus on improving 'pupil engagement in learning'. Engagement in learning is an intuitive concept, one that teachers have a sense of, and which they sometimes overtly strive for. In this way, this is a pedagogically strategic starting point, because teachers can make direct use of a focus on engagement to monitor and adjust their practices. Their own experiences are relevant to identifying groups of learners whom they see as disengaged from learning, and they are in a position to explore this disengagement together, through research and discussion with critical friends. Frequently, and significantly, they discover that there is more going on than they had appreciated – and importantly, this often gives them some purchase on what they should or could go on to address. But this is something that emerges, rather than being straight-forward and easy to create or develop through a rational plan.

Pupil engagement though is a double-edged notion. In one sense all monitoring of pupils in schools has to do with their engagement: discourses of approval and disapproval are mechanisms designed (however crudely) to promote conformity and acceptance of the status quo by pupils, and thereby gain their compliant engagement with the system as it is, whatever the embedded injustices and unnoticed barriers they face. Here we borrow again from Fielding's (2006) notion of person-centredness, to define the engagement of a person in learning as the consequence of an emerging fit between their interests, biography, motivations and issues, and the learning opportunities on offer. Engagement in this sense is not primarily about time-on-task and pupils getting their heads down. Addressing engagement serves inclusion to the extent that young people can make stronger connections between their life within and beyond the institution of the school.

This focus on engagement in learning raises many questions about the relationship between school and community. It is important to contextualise this approach in relation to a whole swathe of approaches to social change, which begin outside the school, working first within local communities to identify and address the problems that lead to a misalignment among young people and their educational experience. In the next section of this chapter, we briefly review a number of initiatives in England and Wales in recent years which ostensibly take this approach, and consider the impact that they have (or do not have) on teachers and the institution of the school. We will be asking how far these approaches are leading to fundamental change in schools as institutions.

Education and communities – exploring systems

In the previous section we adopted a view of educational inclusion as being about the open-ended education of individuals, in relationship with others, and appropriate to a particular social and historical context. The interlocking but separated contexts of the community or communities in which young people develop and the institution of the school are therefore highly significant. Bronfenbrenner's (1979) picture of the development of individuals taking place within a nested set of more or *less* related systems remains a useful way to reframe our attention from the school as institution, to the young person moving between different contexts, including school. These approaches consistently highlight poverty as one of the most intractable factors affecting educational outcome, given that the system continues to work in the way that it normally does. This impact is significant and hard to reduce:

> There is no single explanation for why learners from poor backgrounds do badly in educational terms. Rather, there are multiple factors implicated at the micro, meso and macro levels. There are no magic bullets that will enable such learners to perform as well and derive the same educational benefits as their more advantaged peers. Instead, what are needed are interventions which address the full range of factors and which operate at all three levels.
>
> (Raffo *et al*. 2007, p. xii)

The most significant recent initiatives in England are widely seen to come under the umbrella of 'Every Child Matters', a long-term programme for whole system change, legislated for in the Children Act 2004, aiming to improve life chances for all children but particularly the disadvantaged and vulnerable. They do this by identifying a set of aspirational outcomes for children under a series of headings (five in England, seven in Wales) which add up to a holistic overview of the healthy development of the next generation.

The Every Child Matters agenda was prompted initially by a failure in child protection with fatal consequences, in which the main issue was a lack of communication between different agencies including social services, health and education, where education was recognised as the service accessed most widely and involving the most sustained and intense contact with children and families (Department of Health and The Home Office 2003). The Laming inquiry and the resulting agenda are associated with the development of new organisational structures, most notably the establishment of 'Children's Services' incorporating education, with the aim of improving collaboration between these different agencies. In compelling closer interagency working, they present opportunities and challenges for all practitioners who work to support young people. Typically however, the collaborative structures focus mainly on individual students, through case conferences and so on, and there is little systemic impact on the services themselves. Full-service extended schools (FSES) have the potential to go beyond this, through the co-location of the different services on one site and the attempt to provide 'wraparound care' for vulnerable young people. An evaluation report to the Department for Children, Schools and Families (DCSF) notes that 'promising partnership arrangements, genuine pupil and community involvement, and strategic initiatives at local level were emerging', and that 'FSESs were impacting positively on the attainment of their pupils – particularly those facing difficulties. They were also having a range of other impacts on outcomes for pupils, including engagement with learning, family stability and enhanced life chances' (Cummings et al. 2007).

In all of this, however, the role of the teacher remains ill-defined. Certainly there are implications for responsibilities in relation to safeguarding processes, and more schools may well become sites for services along the extended school model, but these are peripheral to the teacher's core purposes. Training and Development Agency (TDA) teacher standards in England incorporate the notion of teachers becoming more aware of broader issues, and able to collaborate with other professionals, but again fail to consider any implications for classroom or curriculum practice. In other words, there remains a considerable disconnection between the core role of teachers on the one hand, and emerging modes of collaboration between services around young people on the other. This may be due to the conservative practices of the members of these different professions, and the difficulty of professional collaboration in practice where each works under different conditions, rates of pay and so on. There may be more to it than this, however. Teachers' relative isolation as a professional group may relate to an aspect of teacher identity which is essential to maintaining order in the institution of the school (to which pupils do not come voluntarily). As Lawrence Stenhouse identified a generation ago:

> I believe the most important barrier [to change in schools] is that of control . . . To a considerable extent the control element in the relation of teachers and pupils rests on the teachers' fulfilling the expectations the pupils have about how they will behave; and change also threatens this.
>
> (Stenhouse 1975, p. 169)

Teachers rely on each other to maintain control across the institution, and this naturally has profound implications for their relationships with pupils, but also for their social identity with each other and with other professional groups. There is no acknowledgement of such aspects of professional identity within the documentation around Every Child Matters.

In Wales, a strategic planning process has been set in motion to look at how to achieve for young people a set of fundamental rights modelled on the UN Convention on the Rights of the Child. It will be interesting to see whether a rights-based policy approach leads to a different set of discourses and practices from the aspirational discourse of Every Child Matters (ECM).

To a great extent, the dominant feature of all of these approaches is the persistence of a compensatory model based on the identification and treatment of difference. The most developed parts of the ECM model suggest that it remains a rather traditional one of implementing compensatory measures on the basis of assessment of individual need, with systems dealing with special educational needs remaining intact, for example. Some children and some schools remain 'special'. There is little sign in any of these initiatives of the sort of critically informed stance advocated and demonstrated by Luis Moll (González et al. 2005) or of an analysis informed by critical systems thinking such as that developed by Bronfenbrenner.

Work inspired by the concept of families' 'funds of knowledge' is significant in this regard, in the emphasis it places on teachers as learners, in this case through teachers going to pupils' homes not to discuss problems, but making

> research visits, for the express purpose of identifying and document-ing knowledge that exists in students' homes. . . . We are convinced that these research visits, in conjunction with collaborative ethno-graphic reflection, can engender pivotal and transformative shifts in teacher attitudes and behaviours and in relations between households and schools and between parents and teachers.
>
> (González et al. 2005, p. 89)

Our contribution in this context explores the possibility of teachers gaining a more critical perspective, based on research not in pupils' homes, but through having the opportunity to explore their practice together and the systems in which they work in order to reduce exclusionary pressures and influences. We see our project as one that extends and complements the ECM agenda in a more critical and far-reaching direction, most notably because it extends it *inside schools*. As we will later describe, our approach involved educational psychologists in working with teachers, coming to understand their local contexts, and collaborating to identify starting points for more inclusive practice that were meaningful to teachers. This is an example of multi-agency working, but of a very particular kind: in this case, the focus was on the *teachers' educational practice*. The concept of engagement in learning is one that EPs relate to as well as teachers, which further informed the focus for this collaborative work. The perspectives of pupils that the EP brings are contextualised in a different way to those of teachers. As we will see, the sharing and discussion of these perspectives creates the possibility of a growing and deepening understanding by both teachers and EPs.

The challenge for teachers

Having identified the agenda for inclusion as stemming from fundamental issues as to what it is to be a human person in relationship with others, and considered the need to develop inclusive practice through focusing on an issue of direct relevance to teachers in their classroom work, we have now also established this approach as meaningful in relation to structural change around services for children. As we have noted in much of the discourse associated with these changes, the role of the teacher remains underdeveloped.

It is unsurprising therefore that many teachers take some convincing that what they do in their classrooms is directly relevant to this agenda. It is difficult for teachers to recognise the unintended consequences of their practices, and it is easy to hear the discourse of some of the practices explored in the previous section as pointing away from teachers and towards various types of specialist. It is as if teachers are positioned by other professionals as having a view of their students as pupils rather than as people.

Yet it is teachers who control access to the curriculum; whose assumptions, hopes or fears about young people help to create or dispose of chances for them. If the discourse of inclusion does not impact on the way teachers see themselves and their role, the way they perceive pupils, then how can it ever be regarded as more than a surface-level accommodation? Or to put it positively, inclusion as engaging with pupils' engagement is a radical agenda for schools, precisely to the extent that it promotes changes in teacher identity and behaviour.

Returning to our initial list (p. 4) of what is required of teachers engaging in educational inclusion, we can now identify in more detail some of the challenges teachers face.

Asking questions about how schools could and should adapt to and work effectively with the diversity of their student populations

Asking critical questions is key. On what basis should teachers adapt their practice, if not in relation to what they know about the response of learners? The challenge of inclusion as we have defined it requires teachers' active engagement, because inclusion and exclusion are processes that happen minute by minute and lesson by lesson. It requires teachers to be reflecting on their practice, and adjusting that practice in the light of the response of young people.

It is of little value for teachers to adopt well-intentioned programmes without any attention as to whether they have the desired effect on their pupils. Teachers are used to paying a great deal of attention to pupil attainment in tests, but are less in the habit of looking for the consequences of the changes they make on pupils' attitudes, or in the way they are experiencing the classroom. The need is for critical enquiry into the outcomes of particular changes for students. Many of the projects described later justify the value of this emphasis, and they also challenge the dominant sense of what it is to conform in relation to innovation in the classroom. Often, the most valuable outcome was the change in teachers' assumptions, rather than the change in practice itself.

Finding out about and working with what pupils bring with them to school rather than viewing differences in terms of deficits

What pupils bring with them is a diversity and depth of biography, community and identity about which teachers typically know very little. This ignorance can lead teachers into unresponsive practice, blaming pupils when they cannot or do not respond in the expected way, rather than finding ways to involve and accommodate them in the contexts in which they find themselves. Differences do not necessarily constitute deficiencies, or lead to division. Diversity can be seen as a resource, unless pupils are being assessed and categorised on to a single linear scale. How can teachers adjust their practice to begin to understand that and take it into account in their teaching?

Part of the problem can be seen as one of timescale. The curriculum tends to focus teachers' attention on pupils' achievements in a series of short-term processes. Initiatives such as 'learning to learn' challenge this view, but the discourse remains strong. It is hard enough to shift perspective to see pupils as simultaneously making sense of a whole range of subjects, let alone being able to see them as forming identities as young people occupied in family and community as well as school. Bridging this gap requires either great imagination, or systems which facilitate connections across timescales and between different settings.

More broadly, working as *teachers* with what pupils bring to school is about the need for a relationship between teachers and pupils in which both see themselves as learners, with all that entails:

> Working with young children, good teachers are keenly aware that they might have devastating effects or uplifting effects on their students. Some of these effects last, or at least are remembered, for a lifetime. This first great good of teaching – response-ability and its positive effects – is clearly relational. Teaching is thoroughly relational, and many of its goods are relational: the feeling of safety in a thoughtful teacher's classroom, a growing intellectual enthusiasm in both teacher and student, the challenge and satisfaction shared by both in engaging new material, the awakening sense (for both) that teaching and life are never-ending moral quests.
>
> (Noddings 2003, p. 249)

Taking greater account of the understandings that young people have of school and education, rather than seeking only to engage more young people in existing school practice

This third challenge involves taking seriously the growing maturity of young people while they are at school, and finding ways to facilitate their active contribution as citizens of the school, however uncomfortable that is initially for teachers. It links to pupil voice and the school as a person-centred community, in the hope that teachers can come to 'see pupils differently' by taking seriously 'what pupils can tell us about their experience of being a learner in school' and to 'review and change aspects of school organisation' by finding ways 'of involving pupils more closely in decisions that affect their lives in school' (Rudduck and Flutter 2004, p. 2).

It also links to the teacher's search to create a meaningful context for learning – that is, one that is meaningful to the particular young people she or he is working with. This can involve a whole host of choices, and the creation of silly, memorable or symbolic activities. Building a classroom culture for learning can involve the trialling and establishment of shared signs, symbols, patterns, activities, colours and means of communication. The point here is to learn to see lessons from the perspective of the young people, and to understand what matters and makes sense to them, as individuals, groups and subgroups. A striking example of such a process is described in a recent and thrilling paper by John Elliot (2007, pp. 234–237).

All three of these challenges have implications for the relationship between teachers and pupils. Pupils in our study repeatedly high-lighted their appreciation of and positive response to a relationship of care with their teachers, one that goes beyond a young person as a learner of a subject:

> When caring is used to describe a particular sort of relation, both carer and cared-for make significant contributions to the relation. The carer attends – listens to the expressed needs of the cared-for – and responds in a way that either satisfies the need or explains satisfactorily why the need cannot be met. In the latter case, a continuing effort is made to maintain a caring relation even though the immediate need cannot (or, perhaps, should not) be satisfied. The cared-for, in turn, contributes by recognizing the effort; he or she feels cared for and reveals this recognition in some form of response. Then, and only then, does a caring relationship exist.
>
> (Noddings 2001, pp. 35–36)

The particular challenge in secondary schools

If inclusion requires in various forms a relationship of care between teacher and pupils, then the secondary school as an institution presents considerable barriers to the achievement of such a relationship. The complex social and organisational structures of secondary schools have developed over time for a host of unrelated reasons, but they continue to influence the organisational, personal-social and pedagogical ways that schools operate today, which in turn constitute the roots of the dilemmas, tensions and contradictions faced by staff and pupils. Allan (2003) looks at barriers to inclusion in the context of two state policy initiatives (in Australia and Scotland) in which the inclusion of all children was really at issue, and concludes: 'I have argued here that barriers to inclusion extend beyond school systems and include ways of knowing (special education); ways of learning (to be a teacher) and ways of working (within accountability regimes)' (p. 178).

The identification of these three types of barrier remain useful, although we are employing a broad definition of inclusion, rather than one limited to special educational needs. We can identify several barriers to inclusion under these headings, which are factors to be considered in secondary schools, based on our experience and other research.

Ways of knowing

Here we consider the rules that operate to match the curriculum with individual pupils, such as methods for meeting additional or different needs, and grouping according to ability or achievement. A simplistic concept of ability remains one of the dominant sorting variables in most secondary schools. The concept of ability continues to underlie success and failure at school, partly because it is 'propagated . . . by powerful vested interests' (Thomas and Loxley 2001, p. 143) but also because it is taken for granted by many within and beyond education.

Ways of working

Organisational issues present a major barrier to inclusion in secondary schools: the divide between academic and pastoral responsibilities; the number of pupils a teacher sees each week; the separation created between professional colleagues owing to subject specialism, or between teachers and other adults such as support staff, through the lack of time to establish effective collaboration.

The subject departmental structure in itself also presents possible difficulties, in that departments are usually sufficiently separate to maintain different approaches towards staff and pupils. Researchers have found departments to have a great influence on the use of strategies for inclusion:

> Teachers reported a high degree of familiarity with and use of these strategies, however, there was variation between teachers

of different subjects in the extent to which they use some of the strategies. . . . The training of teachers is organised on a subject basis and most secondary schools are organised into subject departments which have different histories, varying degrees of autonomy and different priorities. All these factors produce a range of subject and department 'cultures' that may have an impact upon teacher practice and their views about what works in promoting inclusion. These differences in the use of various teaching strategies between subjects have implications for the nature and organisation of learning support within and across inclusive settings.

(Florian and Rouse 2001, p. 404)

This is not necessarily a problem, but it does suggest that inclusion needs to be addressed at the level of the subject department, not just at the level of the whole school.

In addition, there are the many and often only partially compatible agendas which schools have to address, many of them located within the twin and often contradictory agendas towards inclusion and raising standards.

Ways of learning to be a teacher

Barriers here include patterns of professional practice that have emerged including the culture of professional individualism and the focus on the development of pedagogical skills over educational values. Another challenge is represented by the multi-voicedness of the large community of teachers and pupils.

Allan's (2003) analysis of barriers helps to suggest why inclusion in secondary schools is generally a greater challenge than in primary schools in England and Wales at this time. Competition between secondary schools, particularly in urban areas, adds power to accountability regimes; the pupil differences which fuel the demand for special educational provision are greater at secondary age; and teachers have much less connection with parents and are more oriented to subject demands. Although these features do not necessarily act as barriers, they can create conflicting tensions when trying to develop greater inclusion. Allan (2003) suggests that it is of value to explicitly articulate these 'double edged responsibilities' and she poses them as a series of reflective questions. For example:

'How can teachers be supported in maximising student achievement *and* in ensuring inclusivity? . . . What assistance can be given to teachers to enable them to deal with the exclusionary pressures they encounter *and* avoid becoming embittered or closed to the possibilities for inclusivity in the future?'

(Allan 2003, p. 177)

This emphasis on the recognition of tensions echoes the analysis of Clark *et al.* (1999). Based on an in-depth study of four secondary schools, they highlighted the dilemmas that those schools dealt with and the ambiguities of their practice in relation to notions of inclusion. Many other commentators and researchers have testified to the challenges that secondary schools face in becoming more inclusive. Avramidis *et al.* (2002) studied a school recognised to be inclusive by its LEA and found that 'participants were enculturated into the integration model' and that there was at least some evidence of the social exclusion of 'included students', indicating the need for 'restructuring of the physical environment, resources, organizational changes and instructional adaptations' (p. 143). Carrington and Elkins (2002) describe the complexity of translating inclusive policy into culture in a secondary school, which for their participants included 'collaborative problem solving, inclusive beliefs, commitment to reflection, vision and change, and planning and teaching for diverse learners' (p. 51).

In our project, we found that inclusion was a well-known concept to teachers, whose definitions accorded well with those of the researchers and project leaders. They talked about inclusion as a right for all pupils, in a way typified by the following definitions:

> 'Allowing all students to access the curriculum at a level suitable for them; the access must be real in lessons, not just on paper' (teacher, Hightown science)

and

> 'Inclusion means involving and engaging all (or the vast majority) of students in a meaningful and relevant curriculum. However this may involve considerably differing curricula for different students' (teacher, Hightown science).

However, when it came to deciding what to do differently in the classroom, these definitions proved broad and amorphous, and difficult to translate into practice. What is needed is a way for teachers to learn how to practice more inclusively.

Conclusion

From different points of view, inclusion is about reducing barriers to achievement and participation for *all* learners (Booth and Ainscow 1998); it draws on principles of equity and equality of opportunity (Roaf and Bines 1989); it involves scrutiny of the curriculum but also of the wider social context of learning (González *et al.* 2005), and it is about changes in the learning culture of schools and classrooms (Benjamin *et al.* 2003). Each of these perspectives resonates with the contexts of secondary schools in different ways: the first raises the contradiction of mass education for individuals (Skrtic 1991); the second highlights the difficulty of translating values into practice in a complex organisation; the third raises the issue of communication and connection between community and school, and between teachers and parents, for example, while the fourth indicates the need for deep cultural change involving core school processes (Kugelmass 2004).

Each of these perspectives on the difficulty of achieving inclusion in secondary schools suggests a different route to resolving the central dilemmas with which many of these schools are grappling. But what is common to all of them is the necessity for teachers' active engagement in addressing and working with these dilemmas. As far as pupils and parents are concerned, it is teachers who represent and constitute the school organisation and embody educational values, whose understanding of pupils determines so many possibilities for pupils to engage or disengage, and whose practice shapes the context for learning. Besides, many other significant features of school, such as assessment, curricula and social life, are themselves mediated largely by teachers. Teachers who understand their own significance to pupils' experience know that they profoundly affect the way such features are interpreted and understood by pupils, and that while they cannot change everything, there is a lot they can do to make education more accessible and meaningful.

The implication of this is the need to build up practices in schools which contribute to that engagement by teachers, out of which can come teacher identities of agency, and a hopeful, practice-oriented discourse of inclusion. This is not something that can be established at a stroke; engagement emerges along with a sense of agency, and an opportunity to make meaning together.

Part II

What does the research tell us?

Chapter 2

Teachers are the solution

> In this chapter, we aim to identify the features of teacher professional development that are likely to support the development of more inclusive practice, and those that are not. We begin by considering the characteristics of professional development that promote inclusion, where inclusion is seen as essential to the education of the individual. Bringing this about consistently in secondary schools involves developing more responsive and supportive structures and processes, and teachers engaged together in ongoing professional learning in context. We then evaluate common approaches to teacher professional development in relation to inclusion, including workshops and courses, whole school approaches, mentoring and coaching, development of the reflective practitioner and collaborative approaches. Finally we consider the evidence for action research as an effective and perhaps necessary approach to teacher development for inclusion.

Teachers know how much difference they make to young people. They see it reflected in the efforts and energy that go into the school inspection system, and in the noise that the media make when some teachers withdraw their labour for a day. They detect it in the systems that operate to train teachers, and in the selection, appraisal and promotion systems that aim to reward good practice. They hear it in the talk that goes on in schools about assessment for learning, visual-auditory-kinaesthetic learning (VAK), learning outcomes, lesson structures, curriculum review, and about the countless initiatives that descend on schools in the form of educational challenges, targets and improvement partnerships.

Most of all however, teachers experience their own impact in their lessons. They know how it feels when a class is engaged and focused, or when a pupil lacking in confidence gets praised for a good effort. They know that, in the end, nearly all attempts to improve schooling come down to the way pupils relate to their teachers and vice versa, and whether the relationship is one through which learning takes place. They know they need understanding and answers to questions such as: what makes a pupil choose to try, to engage, to take seriously – or to give up and look for a diversion?

But knowing that one makes a difference and having ownership of one's professional development are two different things. In the next section we build on the arguments of the last chapter in considering the characteristics of professional development which promotes inclusion.

Professional development for inclusion

In this section we consider teachers' development in relation to inclusion from three angles. We look first at the nature of professional development generally; second at the challenge that is involved for teachers in addressing inclusion, and third at the place of values and beliefs in the way teachers develop their practice.

Exploring the nature of teacher professional development

What does it mean to be professional as a teacher, and what does it mean to develop that professionalism? We see questions like these as arising within a social and historical process. From this perspective, teachers, pupils and schooling are not accidental elements in our society – rather, their role and the form they take in contemporary society is the product of a dynamic and ongoing series of developments of which change in schools is only one part:

> Because human labor inevitably entails collective efforts of people acting together, its development gives rise to increasingly complex social exchanges among people, and to individual mechanisms allowing for these exchanges to be carried out . . . the social relations among people become institutionalized in relatively stable forms ranging from the rules of conduct and cognition, such as rituals and morale, to collective forms of life such as state, religion, schooling, and family, that is, the society itself.
>
> (Stetsenko 2005, p. 73)

From this broad historical perspective, the ongoing development of schools and of the role of teachers and pupils is not a matter merely of technical or professional change, but one of many processes that are influenced by (and equally, can influence) the collective develop-ment of human activity, linked to emerging economic relationships and changing cultural norms. Many studies over recent years have demonstrated how dominant approaches to teachers' professional development align with wider changes in societies (Stenhouse 1975; Hextall *et al.* 2007). They illustrate, for example, the dramatic effect of increasingly tight regimes of professional accountability (O'Neill 2002) on notions of teacher professional development. In a recent review of changing teacher roles in Europe over the past ten years, Osborn (2006) notes a shift in the UK away from a 'professional covenant model' towards a 'contractual performance model', with an associated change in the concept of teacher professionalism. In Table 2.1 we

Table 2.1 Teacher development models

	Professional covenant model	*Contractual performance model*
Teacher professionalism	Professional covenant based on trust, and commitment to education as a form of personal development. Confidence, sense of fulfilment and spontaneity in teaching.	Professionalism as the fulfilment of a contract to deliver education, which is seen as a commodity for individuals and a national necessity for economic growth. Less confidence, fulfilment and spontaneity in teaching.
Teacher development	Growth of understanding, role and judgement; an emergent and expansive learning process (Furlong 2000).	Meeting progressively more challenging standards through the demonstration of competence, across a range of pre-specified themes.
Aim	The 'person-centred school' (Fielding 2006).	Performativity: the 'high-performance school' (Fielding 2006).

Source: adapted from Osborn (2006)

have added an outline of the associated shift in the notion of teacher development.

> Teaching as an activity now comes with a much stronger official frame around it. We have argued that this takes the form of firmer definitions as to the purposes of teaching, clearer specifications of the what and how of teaching, more rigorous and assertive vetting and regulating procedures, and a 'fixing' of positions and functions within the structure of the occupation. In short, teaching has become much more tightly bounded, and this tighter bounding is externally defined and imposed.
>
> (Mahony and Hextall 2000, p. 84)

Our contention, in line with our arguments in Chapter 1, is that the characteristics of the professional covenant model must form the basis of professionalism with regard to educational inclusion. Inclusion requires teachers with an orientation towards pupils as persons, rather than as performers; and the education of persons leads to unexpected outcomes for both teachers and pupils. Teachers need to be responsive to pupils, and to see themselves as co-learners in terms of all that young people bring to school. Education cannot be commodified, because it depends on a relationship of care between teacher and pupil (Gilligan 1982). Professional development is emergent and expansive in that the process and outcomes of that development depend on the persons involved, in all their diversity and variety of experience; they cannot be pre-specified.

This model of professionalism has implications for the development of teachers. First, professional development for inclusion cannot be 'bolt-on', because it entails deep change in teachers' practice where that is understood as a developed and habitual mode of activity influenced by social norms, individual dispositions and material circumstances. In a highly referenced extract, MacIntyre (1984) defines practice as a purposeful and expansive activity:

> any coherent and complex form of socially established cooperative human activity through which goods internal to that form of activity are realized in the course of trying to achieve those standards of excellence which are appropriate to, and partially definitive of, that form of activity, with the result that human powers to achieve excellence, and human conceptions of the ends and goods involved, are systematically extended.
>
> (MacIntyre 1984, p. 175)

On this definition, practice leads to the development both of the indi-vidual *and* of the activity in which he or she is engaged. Furthermore, it is expansive in terms of the way outcomes are perceived and inter-preted, as well as in terms of the skills, knowledge and understanding required. It necessarily involves the community of persons, living and dead, who engage in or have engaged in that practice; and it is open-ended in its possibilities. We can link this with a widely quoted definition of pedagogy:

> [T]he act of teaching together with its attendant discourse. It is what one needs to know, and the skills one needs to command, in order to make and justify the many different kinds of decisions of which teaching is constituted.
>
> (Alexander 2004, p. 5)

Together, these definitions of teacher activity as practice and pedagogy highlight its necessarily communal and discursive nature. To know, and to make and justify decisions about teaching, involves participation in a community. Shulman's (1987) well-used concept of pedagogic content knowledge (PCK) as the 'blending of content and pedagogy into an understanding of how particular topics, problems, or issues are organ-ized, represented, and adapted to the diverse interests and abilities of learners, and presented for instruction' (p. 8) further extends this sense of teaching as an expansive, collaborative, discursive practice.

The problem with much teacher development activity is that it takes place without regard to the nature of teaching as practice in this sense. Sometimes that may be appropriate in a limited sense, for example, where changes are made in practice to comply with a regime of external accountability, such as in England with some elements of the KS3 strategy. Such changes can however only serve the cause of educational inclusion by chance. In contrast, developing more inclusive practice represents a deeper, cultural transformation (Zollers *et al.* 1999; Kugelmass 2004) – precisely because of the nature of teachers' professional practice. Based on extensive empirical research, these authors argue that sustaining inclusion is more than a technical issue – it is a cultural one, where significant practice is embedded and justified in the understandings and discourse of a group, and is meaningful to that group. This suggests that enquiring into change towards more inclusive practice must go beyond descriptive questions such as 'What are the teachers doing?' and 'Are they doing things differently now?' Such enquiry needs also to probe into the discourse and community behind teachers' actions, with questions such as 'Do they judge differently? Do they talk differently about mistakes? Do they deal differently with disagreements? Do they deal adequately with challenging information? What do they really care about?'

In her extended case study of an inclusive school, Kugelmass (2004) draws the following conclusion about the significance of culturally embedded practice, when she reflects on her largely groundless fears for the school as the headteacher left: 'I hadn't yet grasped the significance of teachers' collegial commitments, relationships with one another, and deep levels of caring to the school's development' (p. 100).

Many policy documents relating to professional development make assumptions about teachers and their community which reinforce the lack of understanding to which Kugelmass draws attention. Ball (1997) draws attention to the way in which teachers are characterised in two-dimensional terms, disconnected from what it is to be a professional person in a particular context.

> Clearly, in some policy research there are no people as such. There is a deafening silence at the heart of these busy, abstract, tidy texts. Both the people that 'do' policy and those who confront it are displaced. And yet, alongside this, in many 'implementation' studies a 'peopling' is implicit. A set of recalcitrant, conservative and narrow-minded 'practitioners' is conjured up. They hide behind their closed doors, resisting change, maintaining their naive commitments to progressivism, or anti-racism or class teaching (when they 'should' be doing investigations) or group work (when they 'should' be class teaching). Thus, Hargreaves (1996), in reproducing a typically one-sided imagery, quotes four grounds which Cox asserts that teachers use to justify their practices-tradition, prejudice, dogma and ideology. In other studies, of a different sort, equally shadowy characters emerge, romantic resisters, Althusserian 'heroes' (sic) striving against oppression or the 'bad' practices which policy-makers seek to foist upon them.
>
> (Ball 1997, p. 270)

Ball's analysis of the way policy research treats teachers applies also to much educational policy. But if we accept that changing practice and challenging embedded assumptions entails more than technical change, then that means acknowledging teachers as people first, embedded in a network of relationships at work, with individual and shared concerns, commitments, hopes and fears. It also entails acknowledging differences between teachers in terms of their stage of life and career, biography and subject. As a recent questionnaire revealed,

> [S]ome teachers feel negatively about CPD because they feel, with some justification perhaps, that their particular subject interests are never centre stage (and this can operate across phases). By contrast negative feelings are also commonly associated with standardized CPD provision which does not take account of what teachers feel they already know. This relates again to the importance of effective needs identification processes. Positive feelings about CPD (for all but the late career teachers) are quite often, associated with a reasonably clear sense of career progression possibilities, to which CPD opportunities have been and can be linked.
>
> (Hustler *et al*. 2003, p. 152)

The emphasis here on teachers' experience and career expectations further underlines the idea that teacher professionalism and professional development for inclusion is or should necessarily be situated and interpreted within a community of teachers engaging in discourse about their practice.

The challenge of teacher development in relation to inclusion

More briefly but equally critically, professional development for inclusion involves teachers in challenging the constraints around their practice, even while they themselves are subject to those constraints. Teachers taking action and challenging the expectations and assumptions which constitute the status quo, for example, do so while also being subject themselves to those culturally embedded expectations and assumptions. An obvious challenge to be made in relation to inclusion is to the positioning of young people as pupils without a voice. For many teachers, the experience of listening to and learning from young people is a profound experience of professional development which enriches their understanding. At the same time this experience challenges the taken-for-granted rules about speaking and listening that operate in the school. Learning from young people, or from teaching assistants, parents and junior colleagues, for example, is not just a source of ideas and understandings for teachers, but also in itself a process of constructing a more inclusive community of learners, owing to the change of positioning that it entails. This is just one example of many challenges that teachers may face and address.

Values in relation to professional development

Professional development for inclusion involves a discussion of values. We are drawn to a principled definition of inclusion, and a view that inclusion necessarily involves working out those principles in practice. It is an attractive idea, in that it provides a critical framework to evaluate current policy and practice. Principles are easy to state, hard to belittle; contradictory aspects of practice are easy to identify, and alternative approaches are easy to sketch out in principle. This approach is perhaps especially attractive for critical observers standing somewhat outside the system. The more demanding the list of principles appears in a particular context, the more critical power the observer gains over those involved in that practice. Such critical engagement from people who are not caught up in the day-to-day working of the system certainly has a very valuable contribution to make, in shaping and creating debate which might shift the direction of policy or open up new transformatory possibilities for educational practice and organisation. Some of the more radical approaches within the discourse of 'student voice' advocate just such a role for pupils and students (Fielding and Bragg 2003; Rudduck and Flutter 2004; Thomson and Gunter 2006).

However, it does not necessarily follow that the discussion of values and principles is the most useful starting point for professional development for inclusion. There are two reasons why it may not be so. The first is the question of clarity of practical implications mentioned in Chapter 1. Few people, whether practitioners or not, would disagree that 'education is a basic human right and the foundation for a more just society' (Ainscow *et al.* 2006, p. 2), but the implications of such a statement of principle are not necessarily easy to translate into practice. For example, does education 'as a basic human right' imply that separate educational provision is always to be avoided? If so, what, for instance, are the implications for neighbouring schools with different intakes as a result of diverse economic positions, cultural preferences and norms? If housing markets are influenced by parental aspirations to get pupils into good local schools, should this mechanism be disrupted by, for example, randomising or stratifying admissions? Such questions are not easily answered using the language and concept of rights – and indeed some commentators have noted that the discourse of rights focuses on individuals instead of the value of community, and that, for example, 'contentment and fulfilment having their roots in participation, social connection and relationships with others should take precedence over rights in determining social policy' (Thomas and Loxley 2001, p. 151). In any case, determining the relative value of conflicting rights is impossible:

> The actual contexts of practice – the realities of particular teachers working with particular groups of children in particular schools where particular policy imperatives are at work – are complex and contradictory. Doing the right thing may sometimes involve choices between almost equally undesirable alternatives, and the consequences of actions may be unclear and values may conflict.
>
> (Ainscow *et al.* 2006, p. 26)

The second reason involves a question of position, and what is conceivable for people engaged in a practice. The question here is whether it is possible to remain engaged in practice while continually reviewing that practice in terms of fundamental principles. This is partly a question of what knowledge is appropriate for what purpose. Elliott (1991) looks to Aristotle to identify a distinction between propositional knowledge about practice, and knowledge constructed through practitioners' discourse about practice. On this basis, theoretical knowledge derived from principles of inclusion could be considered an inappropriate guide to practice, because it is not situated in a meaningful context. Fish (1994) makes a similar point: that it is not theorising (from values, or whatever) which counts most in practice. Rather, it is informed analysis, often involving 'employing a set of heuristic questions' (p. 378) and leading to an extension of that practice. For Thomas and Loxley (2007) in the context of special educational needs discourse, for example, 'these theories and models have . . . distracted attention from the ways in which we may use our common humanity to understand others to use our common sense to make schools more humane, inclusive places' (p. 8).

We are arguing here that principles do not necessarily make a good starting point for development in practice. Of course, development will sometimes involve working through the practical implications of adherence to sets of values in practice. Critical incidents occur which involve a struggle to apply different but justifiable values, because many values are justified and make sense in a particular context. There was a striking, though perhaps quite commonly experienced example of this during the project that linked with ours in the Teaching and Learning

Research Programme (TLRP) (Ainscow *et al.* 2006), in which the most principled stand was taken by the two teachers of the deaf in a particular primary school, based on their commitment to providing a good education for those particular pupils. They had established a community (involving pupils, parents and other teachers of the deaf in other schools) in which those values were embedded in a particular form of practice. They considered extended separate provision for hearing-impaired children to be an essential element of an adequate education. Challenging that practice meant challenging the basis of that community, and their judgement about educational value, and this led to some prolonged and heated debate within the wider community of the school. As researchers involved at the time, we failed to draw out this issue of incommensurable values which might have contributed to the accumulated wisdom of the community, and may have avoided some of the bad feeling and sense of betrayal felt by those teachers. McLaughlin (2003) argues that such issues of appropriate knowledge require all the resources available in a community of practice engaged in such a particular setting.

> One of the important contributions that 'communities of practice' make is related to difficulties in articulating educational goods in fully transparent ways, especially when what is at stake is not the articulation of abstract ideals but of forms of action in particular circumstances.
>
> (McLaughlin 2003, p. 348)

In other words, one of the particular tasks of a community is to make reasonable judgements in particular contexts. Again, this is why community is so significant to the development of inclusion.

In summary then, professional development for inclusion needs, first, to take place in a community of practitioners, with all the discursive work and collaborative action that this implies. Second, the process of development has to involve challenge to and by that community in relation to the assumptions and constraints on practice if it is to have any significant impact on the way people think and therefore on the continual making and remaking of responses to particular situations. Finally, it is a process that must involve (but probably not start from) people's principles and values, so that they can continue to make sense of their evolving commitments and dispositions in the midst of change.

Evaluating approaches to teacher professional development in relation to inclusion

What forms of teacher professional development can be adopted which give prominence to the features that we have identified as significant here: considering teachers as persons in community; raising expectations of challenge, and leading into stronger and contextualised understandings of principle? This is to some extent a question of evaluation of the currently available alternatives; and of course the extensive literature on professional development reveals a great diversity of approaches which might be considered. Interestingly, some recent empirical work on the evaluation of professional development has found that schools typically look at its effectiveness by investigating teachers' satisfaction with it using a questionnaire; there is very little knowledge about the effectiveness of professional development approaches in terms of outcomes for pupils (Muijs and Lindsay 2008). Instead of evaluating different approaches by their ultimate outcomes, our approach is to interrogate the theory of change (Connell and Kubisch 1998) that lies behind them, in relation to the features of professional development for inclusion already identified. A theory of change approach involves the attempt to consider and describe how change will occur after an action or intervention, including a description of the issue or problem, key steps in the action/intervention, short-term and long-term outcomes. Thinking through the complexities of a chain of consequences to a long-term objective enriches the participants' understanding of how and why an action should be taken.

Teach teachers new practices: the workshop model

Perhaps the most striking feature of much current educational innovation when considered in relation to inclusion is that it involves approaches which appear to be inclusive in their intent. This suggests a model for the development of inclusion which involves promoting such approaches, for example, through workshops and intensive teaching of how to implement these approaches. From this perspective, there is, for example, great potential for teacher development in relation to effective group work (Blatchford *et al.* 2006); the promotion of pupil voice in school communities (Rudduck and Flutter 2004); and assessment for learning where that involves teachers in monitoring and responding more dynamically to pupils' needs (Earl 2003). In a workshop approach, such agendas can be developed and described in ways that make it clear to practitioners to adapt, monitor and adjust their practice; they can offer clear direction and instructions to teachers. By comparison, the discourse of inclusion appears to stand at some distance from the necessary detail of practical development in class-rooms. The *theory of change* here is that the workshop or other input inspires teachers who go away buzzing with excitement and then put those new ideas into practice in their classroom – a theory that supports the dominant CPD evaluation model of the satisfaction survey (Muijs and Lindsay 2008).

However, these approaches become problematic to the extent that the detail gets in the way of the big picture or overall purpose. It can happen that the package becomes an end in itself, and the larger goal is ignored. So group work may be implemented well, but inadvertently exclude particular individuals; pupil voice strategies may turn into lip-service; and assessment for learning may harden and narrow into a regime of more intensive, albeit classroom-based testing. The principles and values behind the approach can get lost in the specification of the detail. This view is supported by many authors in the area. For example, Hoban (2002) strongly criticises models of professional learning that are mechanistic and that operate on the naive assumption that attending a professional development workshop will lead to changed and improved teaching practice.

Studies also suggest that this type of programme typically overlooks the significance of non-formal learning by and among teachers – in other words it overlooks the role of the community of teachers in assimilating new ideas. Teachers who go away from a workshop inspired also need a context in which to challenge their own understanding of the new ideas and also critique the ideas themselves in their own context; but the community they go back to is unlikely to take on such a role without preparation. The failure is often seen as the teachers, whereas the problem is largely with the assumed model of teacher learning:

> Continuing professional development policies that do not appre-ciate the importance of the non-formal learning will be skewed and hence less effective than their proponents hoped. When it comes to explaining this failure, attention will not fall upon the policies (because it is not understood that they rest on faulty learning theories) but, more likely, upon teachers for failing to be sufficiently clever, conscientious or competent to develop.
>
> (Knight 2002, p. 234)

Training teachers within assumed organisational structures – a policy implementation model

Education policy is (necessarily) based on assumptions about teachers, pupils, school culture and community, though these are not usually made explicit. The *theory of change* behind much policy-led change is that new roles or ways of working can be understood and then implemented, and that they have features which will significantly improve practice in some way. Part of this model involves understandings about subject departments, for example, which are assumed to conform to a particular structure, and to value particular kinds of data, within the overall aim of providing effective education. This approach to continuing professional development (CPD) has directly addressed issues of inclusion through, for example, training teachers to take on particular roles such as that of SENCo or to work effectively with particular groups of pupils. One recent example in England is the SEAL project (DCSF 2008), in which a very well-meaning model of intervention with regard to social and emotional aspects of learning has been rolled out across schools in the expectation that the contexts of implementation will be sufficiently homogeneous to fit with the model. But schools are far from homogeneous. The application of such a model from outside a particular context necessarily requires critical interpretation if it is to be made meaningful in that context. Yet in many cases of training in policy implementation, the invitation to engage in such interpretation is either not made at all, or it is lost amid the signals of status of the 'new curriculum' or 'strategy'. This is the context of CPD in which teachers are most likely to be cast in the role of technicians, rather than educators with responsibility to make sense of new ideas for the benefit of the young people with whom they work. It is difficult to see how this easily serves the development of inclusion.

Systemic approaches

Hopkins (2007) tentatively outlines a different approach again, a strategy for CPD which is constructed within a systems paradigm of school development. Systems theory addresses a need to attend to many aspects of a connected system at the same time, and there is an implicit attempt here to align these aspects so that the systems of education work more efficiently, and to the greater benefit of pupils. Within this approach, CPD is most obviously based in a cycle of professional review in which the needs and skills of individual teachers are identified so that the teachers are then channelled towards CPD opportunities, including coaching and mentoring within the school and beyond.

> At the teacher level, the key source of demand should spring from some form of regular teaching and learning review. These should be focused on day in day out classroom practice, subject knowledge, effective subject specific pedagogy and supported by analysis of rich data on pupil performance. The logic here is that the review leads inexorably on to relevant CPD for the teacher.
>
> (Hopkins 2007, p. 90)

This emphasis on managerially organised and systematic CPD as part of a systems approach to school development is based on a well-articulated theory of change, cogently outlined by Mahony and Hextall (2000) prior to their discussion of the inherent problems:

> It surely makes no sense to have established an overall policy regarding school education without at the same time ensuring that the teaching force is capable of delivering that policy. In order for this to be accomplished, trained leaders need to be equipped with the managerial skills to ensure that the policies will be translated into effective practice.
>
> (Mahoney and Hextall 2000, p. 84)

This is a widely held position in schools, with which many school leaders are probably in sympathy. What is likely to be left out of such an apparently rational formulation is any space for critical professional challenge. The 'cycle of review' approach constitutes relationships of power which make such challenge unlikely. There is little space in such a formulation of CPD for reflection on values: instead, the momentum behind the analysis of the practice of an individual teacher drives the focus towards observable features of classrooms and classroom life, and towards a focus on surface features. Furthermore, this strategy again massively underplays the significance of informal learning, and of informal relationships among staff, in terms of motivation for change or capacity to deal with problems. At heart this is an individualistic model of development which does nothing to build and may even weaken the collaborative culture required for effective inclusion.

Educating the reflective practitioner

Since Donald Schon (1983) elaborated the concept of reflective practice, a strand of teacher development work has flourished around the idea of the teacher as reflective practitioner. This is a focus on the teacher as learner in the context of complex everyday processes, with reflection both during and after engagement with pupils providing a significant route to development. Many researchers and commentators (Goodson 2003) have drawn attention to the significance of teacher learning in the implementation of any movement for change, including inclusion:

> Reforms entail extensive learning. An innovation or an instructional policy cannot be enacted unless several professionals (teachers, administrators, principals), parents and students have many opportunities to learn new concepts, new ways of presenting a learning content, new ways of interacting with students, new forms of professional collaboration, alternative procedures for sharing instructional problems, etc. Although there are still many discussions about teachers' professional development, it is clear that looking at the underlying learning processes and unraveling the structural and cultural conditions favoring and supporting this learning process is a fruitful avenue for a rich discussion about teachers' professional development.
>
> (Vandenberghe 2002, p. 653)

Moon (1999) identifies and analyses reflective learning according to five successive stages: noticing, making sense, making meaning, working with meaning, transformative learning. She maps these into a diagrammatic framework (p. 138), arguing that the earlier stages represent surface learning and the latter stages deep learning, with outcomes which are 'integrated, well-informed and well-structured' representations. In the context of teacher learning, the middle stages of making and working with meaning are particularly interesting. The latter 'could be a process of "cognitive housekeeping", thinking over things until they make better meaning, or exploring or organizing the understanding towards a particular purpose or in order that it can be represented in a particular manner' (p. 139). Much of the work that teachers did in the case studies described later could be understood in this way, as teachers took the opportunity of research to think over classroom processes and represent their thinking to others. Reflective teacher learning can be an isolated process, however, and to that extent may not always facilitate the development of inclusion in a community. The implications of this are considered again in the discussion of action research below.

Collaborative CPD

Concurrently with these approaches to teacher development, the rethinking of teacher professionalism described earlier in the chapter has led to an exploration of the possibilities of teachers learning from and with each other, and understanding that within the framework of CPD (Sachs 2000; Toole and Louis 2002). Cordingley *et al.* (2003) suggest that most studies of collaborative CPD report either processes or impact, rarely both; but that nevertheless there is reasonable evidence that:

> Sustained and collaborative CPD was linked with a positive impact upon teachers' repertoire of teaching and learning strategies, their ability to match these to their students' needs, their self-esteem and confidence, and their commitment to continuing learning and development. There is also evidence that such CPD was linked with a positive impact upon student learning processes, motivation and outcomes.
>
> (Cordingley *et al.* 2003, p. 8)

Cordingley *et al.* (2003) defined collaborative CPD as teachers working together on a sustained basis and/or teachers working with LEA, HEI or other professional colleagues.

In many cases, the emphasis on collaboration in the CPD literature comes after a reflection on the nature of adult learning in a workplace context, with the recognition that, for example, 'we have to move beyond this individual approach because individuals make sense of policy messages and change their teaching practice in conversation with colleagues and in ways that are deeply situated in broader social, professional and organizational contexts (Vandenberghe 2002, p. 654). Collaboration as an adult context for learning is discussed by Smylie, who identifies several conditions which promote workplace learning: '(1) opportunities for individuals to work with and learn from others on an ongoing basis; (2) collaboration in group work and learning; (3) chances to work with and learn from others of similar positions; and (4) variation, challenge, autonomy, and choice in work roles and tasks' (Smylie 1995). The first three of these conditions all emphasise the significance of processes which involve people not just as individuals but as colleagues.

One way to learn more about collaborative processes is to focus on the way people talk together, and how that talk leads to or entails the construction of knowledge. A study by Orland-Barak (2006) draws on data from conversations in a group of teacher mentors over a period of time, exploring the dynamics of their conversations and their potential for constituting opportunities for learning. She identifies three forms of dialogue 'in action': convergent, parallel and divergent:

> In 'convergent dialogues' participants mediated understandings that converged into learning about possible solutions to a particular dilemma in mentoring. 'Divergent dialogues' featured participants' use of the conversation space to depart from their personal contexts of mentoring in order to explore, compare and make connections across practices. In these dialogues participants shifted the focus of the conversation to issues outside their particular contexts, engaging in a kind of theorizing about mentoring. In 'parallel dialogues', participants used the conversation space as a setting for developing their own ideas in a kind of 'dialogue with themselves'. These dialogues provided important opportunities for participants to discriminate and dispute their own ideologies and fixed assumptions.
>
> (Orland-Barak 2006, p. 13)

These three forms of dialogue mirror the differences in processes that might typically be characterised (in order) as problem-solving, exploratory and reflective. What might be developing here is a language for some significant aspects of collaboration, the talk, around which it has been difficult to focus. There are strong links here to the language of challenge with regard to assumptions:

> [I]n any one conversation we can identify various forms of dialogue, each of which can be potentially valuable for examining either instrumental or conceptual aspects of professional practice . . . divergent and parallel dialogues can constitute important opportunities for learning because they prompt a discourse in which professionals expose, scrutinize and contest deeply ingrained assumptions about their practice.
>
> (Orland-Barak and Tillema 2006, p. 2)

If the development of inclusion requires the development of such challenging talk between teachers, then it is also clear that this will not happen by chance. For Orland-Barak (2006) there is a need to pay attention to the 'critical role that the facilitator plays in being attentive to the competing discourses that emerge in conversation and how these shape its development into either convergent, divergent or parallel dialogues' (Orland-Barak and Tillema 2006 pp. 2–3).

The significance of the facilitator is very much borne out in the present study, as later chapters will demonstrate. On the facilitator hangs the depth and quality of collaborative process, and the momentum generated in individuals and groups towards more inclusive education.

A final question in relation to collaborative CPD is the nature of the group that is to collaborate. In the secondary school context, the question is akin to one posed by Siskin and Little (1995): 'If we seek to reinvent or transform secondary schooling, would we be wise to strengthen departments, or to abandon them?' (p. 2).

In Siskin and Little's (1995) study, the issue of whether to focus change on departments or to promote change by weakening departmental structures comes down to whether they exist as communities of learning or non-learning. That is to say, there is a recognition that some departments act to repel initiatives for change and to maintain an unhappy status quo with regard to pupil participation and engagement, while others work effectively to engage teachers in development.

Networking

There is a further contemporary approach to teacher development to explore, which involves the concept of the network. Network culture has permeated policy in England and Wales as a central plank of neo-liberal policies and practices (Calder 2003). As Newman (2002) describes: 'Networks and partnerships, public participation and democratic renewal, are all symbols of what has been termed a new form of governance in the UK' (p. 7). This discourse is evident right across New Labour's agenda, involving 'The development of a more consultative process of policy formation, a focus on joined-up government and partnership and the extension of public participation and involvement in decision-making' (Newman 2002, p. 7). In the organisation of local government too, New Labour has encouraged 'flexible local networking (including policy experimentation) as part of its more collaborative ethos' (Painter and Clarence 2000, p. 479). Specific examples include the policy action teams set up by the Social Exclusion Unit, zonal initiatives on health and education, Sure Start, initiatives on crime and disorder and local regeneration.

The relevance to teacher development lies in the idea that knowledge relevant to teaching can be networked, so that it flows freely to wherever it is needed:

> Now we have a new concept of knowledge and of its relation to those who create and use it. This new concept is a truly secular concept. Knowledge should flow like money to wherever it can create advantage and profit. Indeed knowledge is not like money, it is money. Knowledge is divorced from persons, their commitments, their personal dedications. These become impediments, restrictions on the flow of knowledge, and introduce deformations in the working of the symbolic market. Moving knowledge about, or even creating it, should not be more difficult than moving or regulating money.
>
> (Bernstein 1996, p. 87)

It is certainly tempting to believe that useful knowledge can be created in a school, then separated from the creators and their commitments, to travel on to other places where it can be put to use. It is easy to see the attractiveness of such knowledge networks to those who have or assume responsibility for engineering greater equity in mass educational systems, if they make the assumption that knowledge relevant to changing educational practice can also travel in this way. Networks have become particularly attractive in an English educational context, where there are massive and often local inequities represented by the startling variation between schools (Lupton 2006), and where there are few other imaginable mechanisms to achieve this more even spread of developmental knowledge. Networking, it is hoped, can lead to greater equity in a system through a relatively decentralised flow of knowledge and other resources, managed through relationships which are themselves constructed through the networking activity.

Superficially then, the development of networks to address teacher development makes sense. Networking has become a very attractive process in education (Frankham, 2006). It has been at the heart of the rhetoric around several central interventions in England in the past five years. Perhaps the most substantial of these was between 2002 and 2006, when 'Networked Learning Communities' were established by the National College for School Leadership (NCSL), involving 1500 schools. The concept of networking among each individual group of (typically) five to seven schools was employed, in the hope that solutions developed in one group would be made available to other schools, which it was hoped

> should be able to understand and interpret these solutions and transpose them into their own contexts. In this way, network-based forms of organization are seen to carry the potential to accelerate knowledge creation and innovation right across the education system—to make learning and the resultant knowledge widely available.
>
> (NCSL 2004, p. 3)

Up until this point, the discourse of 'learning networks' is 'the discourse of the commodification of knowledge, of its easy transfer across domains and of claimed future benefits' (Frankham 2006, p. 672). In a series of publications, the leaders of the NCSL initiative outline clearly the expectations placed on networks, within a system that is struggling with both the limits of top-down target-setting and also a distrust of the autonomous development of teachers and schools:

> One familiar response to this difficulty has always been that government should 'trust the professionals'. Many teachers still feel that if they could just be left to get on with the job, they would be able to perform successfully. Unfortunately, this is not the case. Teachers, like any other professional group, are just as likely to resort to self-protection in the face of disruptive change as they are to embrace new and better practices. The challenge is to build professional identities and professional learning communities that are oriented towards adaptation and radical innovation.
>
> (Bentley *et al*. 2005, p. 3)

Networking is seen to support teacher development in a middle ground between central accountability and development rooted in local contexts. In relation to inclusion, the danger is that the distance from local context reinforces the tendency to develop rhetoric rather than to take the harder steps of addressing mechanisms of exclusion and marginalisation.

Why action research?

Action research is based on the idea that the potential for change in a workplace can be enhanced through the collective involvement in a project of those individuals who work in that workplace, who have a unified goal, and a vested and serious interest in the project outcomes. It assumes that a momentum for change can be created through the identification of a particular problem and by addressing this problem through a reflective, collaborative process of engagement and critical evaluation, and there is a growing body of literature which provides empirical support to this position. The gaps in that literature suggest that less is known about how to create conditions in the workplace which make these changes more likely, and it is here that we locate this study.

Outlining the field of action research

The term 'action research' has been used in so many different ways that the term has lost some of its original weight. . . . The action research family includes a whole range of approaches and practices, each grounded in different traditions, in different philosophical and psychological assumptions, pursuing different political commitments.

(Reason and Bradbury 2001, p. xxiv)

The family of action research conjured up here is as diverse and at times fractious as most human families. One way to defining action research is to focus on the goal of changes in 'action', where the goal of most research might be 'knowledge' or 'understanding'. Another approach is to see action as central to the method: the means by which understanding and changes in action are brought about. Kemmis (2001) distinguishes between *technical* action research,

a form of problem-solving . . . successful when outcomes match aspirations . . . but such action research does not necessarily question the goals themselves, nor how the situation has been discursively, socially and historically constructed

and

practical [action research which] aims to inform the (wise and prudent) practical decision-making of practitioners . . . much of the action research influenced by the work of Donald Schon (1983, 1987) is of this kind . . . practitioners aim not only to improve their practices in functional terms, but also to see how their goals, and

the categories in which they evaluate their work, are shaped by
their ways of seeing and understanding themselves in context.

(Kemmis 2001, p. 92)

What is often described as an action research 'spiral' fits best with the
technical version: the improvement of practice through a cycle of, for
example, reflection, planning, intervention, evaluation.

But there are other dimensions to action research. One is neatly
summarised by Reason and Bradbury (2001) in their 'three modes' of
action research:

> First-person research practice brings inquiry into more and more of
> our moments of action – not as outside researchers but in the whole
> range of everyday activities . . . Second-person inquiry starts with
> interpersonal dialogue and includes the development of com-
> munities of inquiry and learning organisations. . . . Third-person
> research/practice aims to extend these relatively small-scale
> projects so that . . . they are also defined as 'political events' . . . the
> most compelling and enduring kind of action research will engage
> all three strategies.
>
> (Reason and Bradbury 2001, p. xxvi)

Clearly action research in schools can mean all sorts of things. We know
of action research networks where the emphasis is very much on the
introspective personal development of individual teachers, as well as
projects where the focus is very technical and the application of action
research is a tool used by managers to involve people in a change
process. In the project reported on here we conceived of a relatively
light focus on the individual teacher reflecting systematically on his or
her own practice, and relatively more on second- and third-person
research. The distinction between technical and practical research was
helpful too, and we saw the development of inclusion as requiring action
research with a strongly practical intent.

Creating conditions for action research

Returning to the question of how to create conditions where such an
approach could flourish, we did find some studies giving guidance,
however, on the priorities that we needed to consider. After distinguishing collaborative, individual and instructional accounts of
teachers' learning behaviour as perceived by teachers themselves,
Kwakman (2003) concludes that:

[I]nterventions have to be directed specifically towards designing the working environment as a learning environment for teachers. Such interventions do not address particular learning events organized by staff developers, but concern structural and cultural changes within schools that provide time and stimulus for those activities that are characteristic of strong professional communities, such as interaction and reflection (Hargreaves 1997). So, it is strongly recommended that researchers and staff developers collaborate with schools and teachers in jointly designing and creating those interventions and in investigating their effects. Only when we know more about how these interventions affect learning will we be able to judge the potential of teachers' workplace as a setting for learning.

(Kwakman 2003, p. 168)

Bringing about structural and cultural changes in schools is clearly far from straightforward. Action research is explored in this study as an approach likely to generate such changes, particularly where it is carried out in a way which embodies the constructive elements of other ways of going about CPD examined in the previous section. So from the workshop model we take the ideas of a common starting point and a sense of shape to an intervention, about which teachers can speak with each other. From policy implementation we borrow the value of visibility, the importance of generating a momentum through shared expectations and an agreed process. Systemic approaches are a reminder of the need to consider how a small project sits within and contributes to the larger whole. Reflective learning by individuals is necessary, but it is much more likely to contribute to significant change when it is part of a collaborative process. From networking we borrow the stimulation afforded to practitioners when they encounter other possible ways of doing things.

Engaging in action research clearly has the potential to affect teachers as persons, in ways that may run counter to the development of inclusion. It is, for example, important to consider the way action research might be understood as an unremitting focus on problems, and therefore embodying a negative view of teachers, as some have argued: 'we argue that the deficit approach which characterises action research is unhelpful to some teachers' (Haggarty and Postlethwaite 2003, p. 423).

It is important also to consider how conditions may contribute to a critical orientation which opens up questions about the status quo, and about what might need to change. Such an orientation could be the basis for understanding action research as a way to develop inclusion. One promising approach in the teacher development literature has been to distinguish the types of knowledge that result from processes of teacher learning, and the images of the teacher's role and development that are associated with them. Elliott (1991) sees action research as embodying an approach to practice-oriented theorising in education, producing theories which

> were not so much applications of educational theory learned in the world of academe, but generations of theory from attempts to change curriculum practice in the school. Theory was derived from practice and constituted a set of abstractions from it.
>
> (Elliott 1991, pp. 5–6)

More recently, a useful distinction has been drawn between different three different types of teacher knowledge:

> [T]he knowledge-*of*-practice conception stands in contrast to the idea that there are two distinct kinds of knowledge for teaching, one that is formal [knowledge-*for*-practice], in that it is produced following the conventions of social science research, and one that is practical [knowledge-*in*-practice], in that it is produced in the activity of teaching itself. The knowledge-*of*-practice conception also differs from the first two in that it does not make the same distinctions between expert teachers ... and novice or less competent teachers. . . . Rather, implicit in the idea of knowledge-*of*-practice is the assumption that, through inquiry, teachers across the professional life span ... make problematic their own knowledge and practice as well as the knowledge and practice of others and thus stand in a different relationship to knowledge.
>
> (Cochran-Smith and Lytle 1999, p. 273)

This is a powerful distinction for the consideration of action research, which as the authors suggest can be carried out with any of these three conceptions in mind. There is a tendency in the doubtful processes of action research to look for expert knowledge to implement, and an opposing and craft-like inclination to see teachers' own ideas as sufficient for their development. The notion of knowledge-*of*-practice is linked directly with an understanding of inquiry as an activity which shapes positions and roles in a fundamental way:

Inquiry as stance is distinct from the more common notion of inquiry as time-bounded project or discrete activity within a teacher education course or professional development workshop. Teachers and student teachers who take an inquiry stance work within inquiry communities to generate local knowledge, envision and theorise their practice, and interpret and interrogate the theory and research of others. Fundamental to this notion is the idea that the work of inquiry communities is both social and political; that is, it involves making problematic the current arrangements of schooling; the ways that knowledge is constructed, evaluated and used; and teachers' individual and collective roles in bringing about change.

(Cochran-Smith and Lytle 1999, p. 289)

There is a possibility that inquiry is not only a *valuable* but a *necessary* element in a school community that aims to be inclusive. From this perspective, changes in what teachers think, do and say are necessary to achieving the goal of inclusion – because teachers' thoughts, words and actions mediate a great deal of pupils' experience of school, for good or ill. Moreover, much of teachers' thinking and practice is *rational* – in the sense that teachers talk and behave as they do for good reasons, embedded within the particular school culture, in their experience of teaching, and in their own espoused values and philosophy. From this standpoint, it is only when teachers have the opportunity to think through and reflect on the effects of their actions that possibilities for change in their practice are created. These changes are often not restricted to the cognitive or rational domain of decision-making. They are about feelings, including frustration, anticipation, curiosity, excitement – even joy.

Within a cycle of action research, habitualised actions can be questioned and discussed. In this sense, inquiry makes more of the teachers' action available for critical reflection, and as a method for teacher professional development it is at the very least compatible with this aim (Stenhouse 1975; Elliott 1991; McLaughlin 2003).

The outcomes of action research that we are interested in include teachers feeling more skilled in terms of personal and professional reflectiveness and collaboration; evaluating their practice and as a result feeling more successful at engaging all pupils. But we are not interested in action research in which the aim is to achieve pre-specified outcomes independent of context. If that was all it was able to achieve, we should regard it as laborious and time-consuming. Rather, we see action research as fundamentally having the flexibility necessary for an emergent rather than planned process – where possibilities open up along the way that could not be foreseen and planned for at the start – and we are interested in the possibilities for the wider uptake of such processes in schools, as alternatives to standards-oriented reforms, for example. This is significant, for the reasons suggested in Chapter 1 about the necessarily open-endedness of educational processes, and the conclusions reached there about the necessarily emergent quality of development towards more inclusive processes. To look at it another way, it is important owing to the nature of learning in complex systems, of which the educational system is one:

> Complex systems are not simply complicated (if they were, then brute force would eventually provide answers). They are indeterminate and non-linear. They are indeterminate in the sense that if we know exactly the state of a complex system now, we cannot predict exactly how it will be at a future time and describe accurately each point in the transition from now to then. The explanation is that there are resonances between elements of the system (which might be particles or people) that are not predictable at the individual level.
>
> (Knight 2002, p. 234)

It is strange to think about the educational inclusion of young people in this way, but the point is important. We see action research as a way to work towards better processes in a system – everyone and everything that makes a school – which is very much more complex than we think it is.

Conclusion

In this chapter we have reviewed the dominant approaches to teacher development. We have explored various approaches to professional development and considered how these fit with an intention to develop educational inclusion. We have seen that action research remains an uncommon approach, because it contradicts the dominant idea of teachers as professionals needing skills and expertise. We have looked at how action research might be ineffective in relation to inclusion, if it becomes formulaic, or does not promote critical thought or creative conversation.

We have concluded that teacher development for inclusion should be emergent, embedding the notion of the teacher as learner, and learning as open-ended, creative and transformative of the person in community. It should include the teacher, so that the teacher also gains the benefit that inclusion offers pupils – to be known, understood as having a particular and special contribution to make, rather than to be narrowly judged, and judgemental. All these factors, we suggest, constitute reasons to explore the possibility of teacher development through action research.

Chapter 3

Action research for inclusion

In this chapter we tell the stories of the teachers' action research projects using the data we have gathered. We describe how the process developed, and its impact on pupils and staff. By narrating and then comparing the distinctive nature of each context and some details of the projects that were undertaken by teachers there, we identify some key issues that both helped and hindered teachers' engagement.

An outline of our research

Case studies which explore teachers' diverse experiences of action research for inclusion are crucial to deepening our understanding of teacher development in this area. The information and experiences that inform the remaining chapters in this book are drawn from the findings of a research project within the ESRC's Teaching and Learning Research Programme (TLRP), called 'Prosiect Dysgu Cydradd' (Facilitating Teacher Engagement in More Inclusive Practice). This project developed out of an earlier TLRP project (Ainscow *et al.* 2006) entitled 'Understanding and Developing Inclusive Practices in Schools' which had involved both primary and secondary schools in three disadvantaged areas in England. That earlier project identified ways of making action research work for institutional change in schools, but the methods adopted had relatively little success at engaging teachers in secondary schools. In addition, the different roles played by university teams influenced the project outcomes in each area (Frankham and Howes 2006), in a way that suggested the critical significance of the role of facilitator in such projects.

In order to build on these findings, Prosiect Dysgu Cydradd focused on the challenge of facilitating teacher engagement in secondary schools. Six schools, each from different local authorities, were selected to provide a range of size and geographical location, institutional experience with action research, and national policy contexts. One school withdrew from the project halfway through, and was replaced with another. The majority of schools were in Wales (five) including two Welsh medium schools. The other two schools were in England. Each school was invited to identify a group of staff to participate in a school project. In most cases this was an existing group of teachers, often a subject department, who then agreed and worked on an action research project with the aim of developing their educational inclusion. To contextualise and clarify the potentially nebulous concept of inclusion in the experience of teachers and learners, these groups were asked to reflect on pupil engagement with learning, to identify an issue facing them relating to this concept, and to make that the focus of their action research. As we discussed in the previous chapter, the concept of pupil engagement is one that has meaning for teachers, inviting them to consider the classroom directly, rather than leaving the classroom out of the picture (which has been an ironic consequence of many inclusion projects).

Throughout the process, the school's educational psychologist (EP) was asked to act as a facilitator and critical friend to the teacher group. Some materials and training were offered to the EPs to help to equip them for this role. The processes that developed in schools, and the factors that constrained and assisted teacher involvement were monitored and studied by the EP and researchers. In order to further refine understanding of these factors, to learn about how to sustain changes in practice and about how to influence the wider school, the whole process was repeated in the schools during the following year, beginning with the identification of a different group of staff.

Prosiect Dysgu Cydradd took place in two successive phases (June 2005 to March 2006 and June 2006 to March 2007), with teacher, pupil and EP data collected for each phase. As a result of the analysis of the findings for Phase 1, new ways of working were explored in Phase 2.

The purpose of the information that was gathered was to identify the issues and challenges that had hindered progress, and the factors that had facilitated teacher engagement with their projects. Teachers' initial knowledge and opinions of inclusion and action research were assessed before school project meetings using two project questionnaires to identify any significant influences on subsequent engagement. Teacher perspectives were also gauged during teacher focus groups, facilitated by the EP. These were organised around a theories of change model (Connell and Kubisch 1998) introduced in Chapter 1, and in this way provided a starting point for teachers to explore ambiguities and untested assumptions in their thinking on the issue they were working on.

Formal interviews and informal discussions were conducted with teachers when researchers visited schools, and on the four networking days involving teachers from the different schools. Video conferencing on these days facilitated contact between Welsh and English groups. At the end of their project teachers were invited to complete a questionnaire which asked them to reflect on the factors that had helped and hindered the approach, the impact on them and their pupils and how it compared with other methods of continuing professional development. Seeking teacher perspectives through their projects provided a rich source of data about their engagement, and what affected it.

Information about the views of EPs was generated during regular project meetings, and supplemented with interviews where appropriate. An EP questionnaire after each phase invited them to comment on the factors that had impacted on the teacher project, the teachers' engagement and their own involvement. This data provided information about school factors at teacher and EP level that affected teacher engagement.

Information about the school context was collected by LA and headteacher interviews at the start of the project and headteacher interviews at the end. Teachers and EPs gave opinions and feedback about school-level factors by their responses to questionnaire items and verbal feedback given during network days and on researchers' visits to school. On visits to project schools, researchers made ad hoc classroom observations, engaged in discussions in staffrooms, and observed interactions between staff and pupils, providing an opportunity to observe how teacher projects were developing in the schools (Table 3.1).

To identify any relationship between changes in pupil responses and teacher engagement, three questionnaires were administered to relevant pupils before and after the teacher projects. In the absence of any directly relevant published instrument to test pupils' assessment of inclusivity of lessons, two related published questionnaires were adopted: the Myself As Learner Scale (Burden 1998) and the Individual Classroom Environment Questionnaire (Rentoul and Fraser 1979), both published in Frederickson and Cameron (1999), and a further

Table 3.1 Characteristics of project schools

School	No. of pupils	Catchment area	Language medium	Pupils entitled to free school meals (%)	Pupils on special needs register (%)	Pupils from ethnic minority backgrounds (%)
Bont	900	Semi-rural	Bilingual – but Welsh mostly spoken	8	11	0. 2
Cwrt	600	Semi-rural	Bilingual – but Welsh mostly spoken	2	34	2
Hightown	1050 (excl. 6th form)	Suburban	English	7	4	16
Main Road	1030	Urban	English	14	27	0. 1
Neuadd	1000	Semi-rural	Bilingual – but English mostly spoken	10	17	2
Parc	1800	Urban	English	6	12	5
Pentre	1400	Semi-rural	English	8	30	2

questionnaire was designed and trialled in the project (What I Think About School (Howes *et al.* 2007)). In addition, pupil focus groups were held with a cross-section of pupils who had completed the question-naires, in which researchers encouraged pupils to consider the impact of teacher projects, and their general perspectives on inclusion.

Teachers evaluated the impact of their projects on pupils in a third teacher questionnaire and during follow-up interviews.

Case studies

These case studies represent the empirical exploration of our theory of change, drawing evidence from participants' perceptions, recorded interactional episodes from discussions, questionnaire results, ethno-graphic observations and so on. They capture the process of developing a school action research project at the micro-cultural level of teacher experience and collaboration, as well as considering the macro-cultural factors that impinge from whole school and wider agendas. These narratives of teacher experience are illustrative of aspects of the school context that can benefit such a process, as well as those that can result in dilemmas and tensions. These case studies have the primary role of elaborating the features of an action research process that is effective in engaging teachers in more inclusive practice. But together, these case studies raise questions: about the extent to which action research can be seen as a rational, planned and systematic activity, for example, and about what is necessary for EPs to take a more systemic role, given traditional expectations of pupil case work. They raise questions about what it takes for action research to be an emergent process, in which possibilities are created and constructed as the process continues – in which surprises happen, in which the facilitator needs to tap into modes of change as they emerge, in which fluidity, learning and alertness to opportunities are central features for everyone involved. The central characters of these case studies are teachers, interacting in various ways with EPs, pupils and senior management.

These eleven case studies are clustered according to whether the action research developed around an issue or an activity. Starting with an activity is a way of working that groups of teachers commonly use – whether it be working with a new curriculum, or a new registration routine, lesson strategy or set of resources. The challenge in starting with activity is to foster a discussion between teachers in such a way that underlying issues can be addressed, with ideas and challenges emerging which further guide development. By contrast, starting with an issue places different demands on the group. It means that the group then has to search actively for and effectively trial a relevant approach. This places demands on the members of the group that they be open first to discussing the issue, and then to identifying a practical way forward.

In each cluster, there is one extended case study providing more detail about the developing process in one of the schools. Detailed stories could have been told about many of the schools, but the decision to describe all school projects avoids a partial focus on those projects that were seen as most successful, or most problematic. In this way, all the experience gained can contribute to a fuller and less selective understanding of the issues of significance for action research to be used in a powerfully developmental way in schools.

Action-focused projects

Trialling the use of pupil whiteboards at Ysgol y Neuadd (Neuadd Welsh project)

A community comprehensive school of approximately 1000 pupils based in a small town in South Wales, Ysgol y Neuadd, accepts all pupils from its community and some who come by choice from beyond. It is a naturally bilingual school with both Welsh and English spoken, although English is the predominant language medium of the school. About 10 per cent of its pupils receive free school meals, 2 per cent of pupils are from ethnic minority backgrounds and 17 per cent of pupils are on the SEN register.

For this school project, volunteers – either whole departments or individual teachers – were sought from the staff. The Welsh department was selected and also one colleague from the English Department joined the group because of her enthusiastic interest. This made a group of seven teachers. Early momentum was lost owing to the absence of the facilitator due to illness but interest was regained when it was decided to trial the use of individual pupil whiteboards during language lessons. The thinking behind this was that it would support all pupils to engage more actively in the lesson as well as giving teachers immediate feedback about which pupils required more teaching input. Discussing how to measure changes in pupil engagement led to some stimulating thinking – How do we know when pupils are engaged or disengaged? How do we measure it? Eventually an observation checklist was developed that was used to measure pupil behaviour before and after one and a half terms of whiteboard usage.

The school management tried but struggled to facilitate sufficient time for this large group of teachers to meet, but did provide material support for the project by purchasing the whiteboards needed for the project.

The facilitator continued to find it hard to find time to hold meetings. When time became short, there was a tendency for the teachers to panic and try to move the facilitator into a more directive role. The facilitator began to realise that she did not have the skills needed and would have liked more support from the university. Despite these difficulties the teacher project was completed and provided some sound evidence that the use of whiteboards kept pupils more focused on the task and able to participate in classroom activity.

Summarising comments: The teachers involved at Ysgol y Neuadd were focused on a particular action to improve engagement in learning. However, in starting to discuss impact, they developed their understanding of what pupil engagement looks and feels like in practice, as well as their classroom repertoires. Action led teachers to reflect on key educational ideas.

Trialling peer mentoring at Ysgol y Pentre (Pentre pastoral project)

Ysgol y Pentre is a secondary comprehensive school of approximately 1400 pupils situated in the suburbs of a town in Southwest Wales. The language medium of the school is English. The headteacher regarded the relationship between the school and the local authority as 'fruitful' and the planning and oversight function of the LEA was valued. The school serves a population of pupils from a wide range of socio-economic backgrounds, although only 8 per cent are entitled to free school meals. There are about 2 per cent of pupils from ethnic minority backgrounds; however, nearly 30 per cent of pupils are on the SEN register.

Interviewed before the start of the project, the headteacher expressed some anxiety that if inclusion meant 'not excluding anyone', and that the school was there to serve everyone in the local community, he was uncertain whether the school was able to meet everyone's needs. The pace of change was perceived as too fast and there was a danger that if a school could not adapt quickly enough it would let some pupils down: 'In schools like this we're seething with things that need to be resolved . . . nothing gets embedded, that's the problem. You can't do it because there's something else coming along that you have to change.'

The teachers who participated in this project also felt burdened with the weight of new initiatives, and there was a danger, at first, that our project was perceived as yet another one of these. They expressed some reluctance after the headteacher selected them to participate. His decision came about as a result of moves within the school that were part of the 2006 remodelling agenda – with the aim that Heads of Year would become facilitators of pupil learning. This was an executive decision on his part, owing to a shortage of time at the start of the project. Being selected in this way was not a good start, and the Heads of Year felt that they had been parachuted into yet another new initiative with little consultation. At the opening session of the project it was evident that they felt a little resentful, unsettled and unclear about control – was it their project? The university's? The facilitator's? or the headteacher's?

This was not a good beginning by the school management in building a supportive relationship with the group. The teachers had immediate concerns about the time needed to engage in this process productively. As a phase 2 project, they had heard about helpful practices in other schools. The teachers identified that the most practicable way to gain time was to follow Main Road's example and request that a common free period be timetabled and safeguarded in order to meet to carry out the project. After some negotiation the senior management agreed to this, and work was able to begin.

As a group they shared a perception that the pursuit of academic achievement was damaging to the school experience of a large number of their pupils: 'When you realise that 40 per cent of all students never get above a C in any subject, you know they fail from day one. . . . School is a brutal place for a ton of people who are not very good at something.'

The pressure for 'results' was also distorting their role as a teacher: 'We're basically GCSE machines aren't we? We bring the kids in one end, we're working as fast as we can to get them out the other end.'

The responsibility of the Heads of Year was to provide pastoral support to pupils. The group shared a passionate commitment to the school's role as a developer of people – including the pupils' social and emotional development. They also shared a fear that this aspect of the school's work was being eroded by the pressure for higher academic standards: 'The TLRs [Teaching and Learning Responsibilities] have sort of dissolved our personal and caring ethos, pushing for achievement.'

This was a group of teachers who knew each other well owing to frequent liaison as part of their pastoral role, but who rarely had the time and space to develop a common piece of work together – so that this project, once time was allocated to it, became a valuable opportunity to do so. The group had previously experimented in a piecemeal fashion with a peer mentoring scheme, and they quickly identified action research as having the potential to allow them to investigate this approach more rigorously. The pupil mentoring system that they wished to pilot linked sixth form mentors with pupils at risk of disaffection in the lower school. The sixth formers who undertook the mentor role were selected from a wider pool of pupils who had volunteered. After a short period of training, the mentors met their mentees two or three times weekly to talk through issues and problems that the mentees were experiencing in the classroom or with their learning. Under the project, the scheme operated for a term and a half before being evaluated.

Given that the selection of project was quite straightforward in this case, the facilitator found that her role quickly moved on to helping the group develop ideas for evaluation of their initiative. After some useful discussion it was decided to measure impact by trying to record changes in pupil self-confidence, particularly in relation to learning. They found the advice of the facilitator, who was experienced in evaluation and assessment, useful in trying to decide how this would be achieved. Eventually it was decided that a published pupil self-evaluation checklist would be used to monitor any changes in self-confidence that might result as a consequence of mentoring.

The leader of the teacher group naturally emerged as the process developed. He was Head of the sixth form, and the coordination of the sixth form mentors was an important part of the teacher project. However he was also someone who enjoyed intellectual challenge and applying this to his work, so his involvement in the action research provided an excellent opportunity for the school to benefit from these talents and abilities. More broadly however, the teachers continued to feel that the school management had not really engaged with the project and did not show interest in its progress. From his point of view, the headteacher reported at the end of the project that he had no detailed knowledge of what had been happening and he had perceived the project as somewhat 'self-contained'. It is interesting to observe that this lack of involvement was construed by the headteacher as positive and evidence of non-interference; whereas the teachers saw it as a lack of interest and support.

The facilitator was viewed by the teacher group as giving excellent support because she provided an organisational infrastructure to their meetings that kept them on track. This was mainly achieved by compiling agendas, keeping minutes and highlighting decisions that required action before the next meeting. Although this activity may be perceived as mundane, it contributed to maintaining the momentum of the group without taking control or ownership. As an external monitor the facilitator also helped to keep the activity of the group going when other competing agendas within the school might have swamped or derailed it.

During the following months the mentoring scheme moved forward smoothly, and the facilitator's role was lower key. For the mentors participating in the scheme it was a valuable experience, and their enthusiasm resulted in the production, with the teachers' help, of a short film recounting the benefit of their experiences. It was also intended that this film might be used to attract volunteers if the scheme were to be extended. The mentees, despite often being challenged by punctuality and attendance, came to most sessions with their mentors, and reported positive views about the opportunity to talk with older and more experienced peers. The formal evaluation provided more mixed results. It would be unrealistic to expect that a mentoring scheme would be effective for all pupils. However, for the Heads of Year this scheme injected back into the school environment more opportunities for pupils, particularly those at risk of school failure, to develop relationships that could support their learning. For the Heads of Year good relationships like these were the 'glue holding things together' in school. This had been the major concern that had underpinned their choice of project, and as a key pastoral team they reflected positively on the way the project had given them the space to work together to develop and evaluate these ideas.

Collaboration had been essential not least because of the coordination between the lower school and the sixth form to make it work. As Heads of Year, these colleagues did meet in the course of their work but they had little opportunity to explore more fundamental issues. Being involved with the project gave 'permission' to take time to share and discuss ideas. For example, what should be the relationship between pastoral work and pupil learning? What should be the important elements of a pupil's experience of school? How to achieve the right balance between raising achievement and developing other aspects of a pupil's development?

At the end of the project the teachers reflected that they had found doing action research a more valuable experience than more usual types of professional development activity – they had appreciated the direct participation, the practical orientation and the potential for longer impact. One of the teachers commented: '[The school is] willing to throw a couple of thousand pounds at a visiting speaker but it would be much more useful spending money giving time to this approach.'

The support of the facilitator was felt to be essential; one teacher went so far as to remark that she had been the 'key to our project'. Although agreeing with this sentiment, another teacher questioned whether it necessarily needed to be an educational psychologist . . . perhaps it could be a senior teacher, possibly from another school?

The Heads of Year anticipated that from this beginning it would be easy to continue to expand the scheme, as the pilot had developed a lot of interest among sixth formers who would be able to take on the mentor role. Interestingly the headteacher also recognised the potential value in the action research method and perceived how it could be used in future. He described it as 'a method that I can give to people who want to do things'.

A strength of the method is that it can be 'given' by the management to encourage teachers as change agents in their own classrooms, their own schools. But to be effective the 'giving' must come with the support from senior management that can make it happen. For example, Ysgol y Pentre management gifted the protected shared free period. A perspective of 'giving away' the method brings with it the danger that the senior management will also absolve themselves of interest and responsibility. If this does occur then the school project may not be completed successfully or there may be a loss to the potential for wider impact and sustainability.

Summarising comments: These teachers at Ysgol y Pentre took the opportunity to explore a way of creating more useful and sustainable relationships between pupils of different ages in the school. They demonstrated that older peers could provide valuable support to pupils at risk of failure. Even more significantly, they strengthened their contribution to the school as a group that cared about and worked for these things. They were aided in this by the active support and encouragement of the facilitator, and by combining their individual strengths as a team. As a result, the headteacher learnt something of the value of giving teachers some autonomy over a project of their own.

Testing coloured filters to improve reading at Ysgol y Cwrt (Cwrt SEN project)

Ysgol y Cwrt is a small secondary comprehensive school of about 600 pupils on the outskirts of a town in mid-Wales, a bilingual school where

Welsh is the main medium for teaching and learning. It accepts all pupils from its community; most have attended a Welsh-medium primary school, but the level of their Welsh proficiency varies depending on the first language of the home. Approximately 2 per cent of pupils receive free school meals, 2 per cent of pupils are from an ethnic minority background but 34 per cent of pupils are on the SEN register.

A teacher who had previously engaged in action research decided to work alongside the specialist support teacher and a support assistant to develop a project together. From the word go they functioned as a relatively autonomous group and did not expect very much from or rely on the facilitator. The support teacher enthusiastically seized the opportunity to lead a project that related to SEN support. It was decided to evaluate the effectiveness of coloured filters in assisting the reading of children including those with dyslexia. The support teacher wanted to pilot this approach in anticipation of rolling it out to the whole school. The level of organisation of the group was impressive. They efficiently identified the reading tests to administer as a means of evaluation before and after a period (a term and a half) of the use of the filters. However, the relationship with the facilitator did not really progress – the time to meet was a challenge to all participants; as a result the group did not meet with the facilitator very often and when they did, the dynamics of their relationship were uneasy. This had at least one consequence which was a loss of facilitation to help the group consider and reflect on their project at every stage.

However, in practical terms the teachers completed their research successfully. The results they obtained were difficult to interpret as the provision of lenses had seemed to benefit some children and not others. This gave the support teacher valuable food for thought and informed her thinking about the use of the method more widely. The teachers regarded the experience as very beneficial – it enabled collaboration between a group of colleagues who traditionally would not have worked together in this way, and they had an opportunity to stand back and look at one area of their work in detail – including acknowledging all its complexities!

Summarising comments: The Ysgol y Cwrt project had a technical focus which the teachers were able to explore without much assistance, strengthening their sense of working together in the process. The results of their evaluation challenged some assumptions and so promoted a more subtle approach towards this resource adaptation, and perhaps to others as well.

Developing a pupil reward scheme at Hightown School (Hightown pastoral project)

Hightown is a 13–18 multicultural school of 1300 pupils, on the edge of a large conurbation in the English Midlands, where there was considerable underachievement associated with a changing pupil intake.

The assistant head for inclusion wanted to use the project to develop the pastoral system in the school, focusing particularly on clarifying the role of the form tutor to be less bureaucratic and more constructively engaged with pupils. The initial focus group involved four tutors and their Head of Year, who engaged very strongly with focus group questions about disengaged pupils. They explored the possibility of changing the reward system in the school rather than trying to improve the already elaborate computer-managed sanctions system picking up low-level misbehaviour.

After another meeting with the EP around the mind map he had created of their focus group discussion ideas, the group decided to explore how form tutors could run a better reward system with their groups and improve relationships with pupils at the start of the day. They elicited pupils' views on the existing rewards scheme using a questionnaire, followed up by some group interviews with pupils. One of the tutors began to take the lead through her commitment and capacity within the role, having all sorts of ambitous ideas about the changes they could make and the activities they could run with the pupils. A Head of Year helpfully brought some balance and realism in terms of workload. The group made an early presentation of their plans to the school leadership and received strong backing, including monetary support for a trip for the form group that earned the most reward points by the end of the term.

Tutors involved in the development of the scheme learned a lot from pupils during the project, not least from the feedback from those pupils who said that they did not need rewards, that they were self-motivated. One tutor had started to 'insist on pupils coming up to speak to me at my table and it's a good chance to talk with them'. Another noted the need to reward the pupils who worked, when pupils commented on 'how they feel bad about seeing "naughty" kids getting rewarded for sitting in their seat – I started to pay more attention to the well-behaved pupils, and less to the others'. The teachers also valued the opportunity to contribute at the whole school level, and to see how the management of the school operated in terms of resourcing and decision-making.

The EP assisted the group in making a statistical comparison between the four tutor groups involved in the 'pilot' and the four not involved, which demonstrated that the project was having an appreciable effect on the number of sanctions that pupils were accruing. This strengthened the move to take lessons from the project about the importance of rewarding positive engagement by pupils, and apply them more widely, with the development of a house system in the school and vertical tutor groups.

Summarising comments: This ambitious attempt to pilot a new reward system at Hightown worked well owing to the combination of energetic and committed form tutors, the involvement of a member of senior staff to ensure resourcing, and the facilitator's ability to assist reflection and decision-making based on evidence.

Issue-focused projects

In this second cluster of projects, the focus was mainly on the issue relating to pupil engagement that the group wanted to address. From that issue, these groups decided upon and investigated the effect of one or more actions.

Increasing pupil motivation at Ysgol y Parc (Parc science project)

Ysgol y Parc is a secondary comprehensive school with 1800 pupils on the outskirts of a city in South Wales, an English-medium school drawing its intake predominantly from more prosperous suburbs. Six per cent of its pupils receive free school meals, 12 per cent of pupils are from an ethnic minority background and 5 per cent of pupils are on the SEN register.

The headteacher selected the Science Department to participate in the project because he wanted to maintain the momentum that had developed from recent changes made there. Three young staff – two quite newly qualified and one with eight years' experience – volunteered to become involved. The more senior teacher emerged as more interested and enthusiastic, and began to organise the other two, becoming the group's leader.

The facilitator, who had worked in the school for many years and who had prior knowledge and experience of action research, guided the teachers through the process. They began with an interrogation of pupil disengagement and, by using theory of change, identified a stepwise change plan. Eventually this included consideration of alternative teaching approaches that could be tested and evaluated. The facilitator described her role as carrying a 'backpack of ideas', from which she provided, for instance, an accessible and relevant article on improving pupil motivation – not leading or directing the group but providing ideas to stimulate their thinking. After a couple of meetings the group decided to incorporate a number of strategies into their teaching that they anticipated would increase pupil motivation, for example, by seeking pupil feedback on the quality of the lesson, and using a positive assessment scheme for marking.

Although the support from the facilitator was regarded by the teachers as 'fabulous, couldn't have managed without her', partly owing to the 'structure, ideas, support, focus' that she gave to the project, the facilitator herself was concerned that she had not done enough to bring the Head of Department and school management on board. The teachers experienced difficulties in finding times to meet, and were given no reduction in other responsibilities (e.g. participation in a departmental review).

The biggest benefit of the project reported by two of the three teachers was a positive change to their relationship with their pupils, and a greater awareness of pupil needs: 'I will be looking at lessons from the pupil perspective in future.'

The headteacher noted that 'participants used the project to enhance their teaching skills and questioned current methods'. Involvement in the group also became a springboard that contributed to a successful application by the group leader to become the school SENCO shortly after the project finished.

Summarising comments: The project at Ysgol y Parc began with analysis by teachers and facilitator around pupil disengagement, and then the selection of teaching approaches that might be more motivating for pupils. For the teachers concerned, the significant outcome was in terms of positive relationships with pupils. However, this project remained disconnected from the wider school and from making a wider impact.

Addressing girls' underachievement at Main Road (Main Road history project)

At the start of this project, Main Road was experiencing a tension familiar to many secondary schools in England. A mixed comprehensive school with 1100 pupils in a large urban conurbation, it was a Leading Edge school, recognised as having the capacity to coordinate and lead professional development. Main Road also had a strong history of inclusion of pupils with special educational needs, with 27 per cent of pupils on the SEN register. Recently however, performance in external exam results had dipped, and the relatively new headteacher was expected to address this urgently.

Action research was not totally new in the school: some groups of teachers, and one assistant headteacher, already had some practical experience. To allocate time for this project, the assistant head invited departments to write a brief bid outlining and justifying the action research project they would run, and the history department was selected from three responses. The school agreed to contribute practically by protecting a period during the week when none of the group were teaching, so that none of the three would be required to cover for absent staff during this time. This turned out to be very helpful.

There were three history teachers, and they got on well with each other: Anne, the Head of Department, was an experienced and dynamic teacher with an open style, keen to gain promotion within the classroom. Chris was more experienced and had whole school responsibility for training new staff. Charlene had been there for two years following her training. Halfway through the project, Charlene left on promotion and Harry arrived, another relatively inexperienced teacher.

The three history teachers had identified a shared, meaningful, relevant and actionable focus for their project: getting girls more enthusiastic about history. Boys, they said, outperformed girls in history, which was unusual, and yet girls were largely ignored as a vulnerable group in the school. The three history teachers also felt somewhat vulnerable, both in the school and in lessons. First, many pupils opted not to continue with history after three years.

> *Chris*: Because it's an option subject we are in, almost you know, we are in market forces . . . as much as we might not like it . . . it is the way of things, so we really do have to market ourselves.

Second, the 'disaffected girls' were causing them some distress in lessons.

> *Charlene*: It almost feels like you could do two identical lessons with two classes and one could be fantastic and one could be rubbish and that's purely dependent on how many disaffected girls there are in the room.

The teachers were assisted in the project by the school's educational psychologist, Matt. He held meetings with them once every half-term, and worked with them in a facilitative style, building relationships and fitting in with their needs. These regular appointments with Matt kept the project moving along.

Near the start of the project, the teachers and Matt elaborated on the issue at hand, which the teachers experienced as demoralising, depressing and difficult.

> *Charlene*: It kind of – degrades isn't the right word at all, I don't think it is, but it affects the lesson, it degrades the lesson . . . it demoralises you, but the lesson – if *they* weren't there . . . normally it would be really effective, but there are enough of them, even though it may only be five of them going [pulls a face and breathes a couple of huge sighs] like that. . . . I find it I find it very depressing really and demoralising when they look at me like that.

The history team were in the habit of talking about their mutual professional concerns in this way. In this project they went further by clearly identifying and working on a focus about which they felt deeply. This strengthened their resolve to do something to address it – but it also heightened their perception of what a complex problem it was for them.

> *Anne*: You are in a difficult position with the parents as well because they're not *technically* doing anything wrong so you know . . . sometimes you get these defensive parents because they're nice little girls who aren't in trouble [*no notes in their books, says Charlene*] there'll be no notes in their books or planners. The book will look *beautiful* because it's all coloured in and gorgeous.

The teachers explained the girls' behaviour by their socio-economic background, but discussions with the EP helped the teachers to be explicit about their thinking, and be challenged by the EP's distinctive perspective:

> *Chris*: The values very often that are shown to this group are the values of the world in which they live. It doesn't matter if you don't get that A* or that B, because you know you'll get by. You'll get help. And it doesn't matter. If it doesn't interfere with the social

life. . . . So it's a dumbing down of practice . . . no incentives to work hard if the parents aren't involved [*Charlene joins in, if the parents aren't involved*] in valuing the education.

The other teachers joined in along similar lines, before Matt caused a pause by saying:

> You see with me, I don't know if *I* aimed much higher than I needed to go . . . [Lots of errrms, hmmms and I don't knows] so a part of me thinks . . . *rational choice* . . . [pause].

Matt's position outside the 'accountability' system seemed to promote a deeper professional discourse within the group. But he was not promoting a grand vision of either action research or inclusion. Instead he worked to normalise both. His listening was significant. He gave value to teachers' deliberations, acknowledging their feelings rather than disregarding them, and then through gentle questions nudged their thinking along more constructive avenues. He helped the group to discuss, decide, take action and consider how to evaluate the effects. Notably, his own involvement and enthusiasm for this process grew along with that of the group.

As a complete department, this was a team with considerable autonomy. Once they had articulated the issue and their target group ('*the underachieving girls in year 8 who keep a very low profile in self-sustaining friendship groups*'), they then identified and listed five girls in each of the four classes. They then settled on two ideas. They created a pupil subject council for history, in which they rigged the election to ensure that their target group of girls were represented. They also set up a fortnightly 'pupil voice box' via which pupils could make anonymous suggestions about improving lessons, 'to help them feel more empowered' (teacher).

These actions were chosen with the aim of increasing the engagement of the girls, giving them a stronger voice in the way history lessons were organised, and contributing to the pupils' sense of ownership. To begin with, the suggestions forthcoming from the pupils were disappointingly narrow.

> *Anne*: What they've been suggesting, is what we thought really they probably would do – you know, more video, more drama, that sort of thing.

These actions appeared to be rather disappointing in their impact. But set within the groups' ongoing attempts at better understanding of the pupils, one thing led to another.

> *Matt*: I was fair buzzing with excitement after the meeting this week with the history group at Main Road – they keep doing interesting things, and there was some really interesting reflection on the whys and wherefores!

The group of history teachers constructed an observation schedule to monitor the behaviour of the target girls, agreeing to sit at the front of each other's lessons observing the pupils. Those observations made a difference.

> *Matt*: They just seem to be . . . well tuned into what the students were actually doing and not doing, and how the group dynamics were working.

But it was not so much what their observations told them, as how the process of observing in this detailed way had changed their thinking about the pupils in general.

> *Matt*: They have become so fascinated by group dynamics that it's in their minds all the time. . . . I think they're . . . kind of doing the things that I think EPs do some of the time, which is to kind of get under the skin of the dynamics in a way that is really helpful, because it will sensitise them to things that are going on without really addressing them all in a strategic way. . . . So it's becoming part of the fabric of their very beings [laughs].

Another enquiry activity was to shadow some of the girls for a day, learning more about how they engage in other lessons like drama, and whether the more active learning is something that they benefit from and therefore might be able to do more of in history. They wanted to know how the different subject and curriculum expectations were met by the way things are organised, as a way of reflecting on their own assumptions about history. In addition, the teachers designed a questionnaire for other staff to find out whether their own observations of changes in the girls were recognised in other lessons.

Teachers' talk changed, away from the tendency to blame the pupils, relying more on evidence.

Matt: In the beginning of their understandings of things, they fell back on those, sort of flighty kinds of things, but now they're looking at a bit more detail about what they're actually doing and not doing.

Working with this group changed Matt. He had come to see the project as a learning experience, and one that pleasantly surprised and enthused him.

Matt: It feels like [I am] creating space and permission for them to behave in ways that maybe motivated them to be teachers in the first place.

During the project, university researchers (Andy and Sam) did little in the school other than to generate data through pupil questionnaires and focus groups. The most active of our roles was as a sounding board for Matt, who was able to explain his changing feelings about the project, and what he had noticed. Two network video conferences were also encouraging to the project team, as a forum where their work was acknowledged in front of peers from the other schools involved.

Over the year, the project brought about several specific and significant changes. Anne came to see action research as way of engaging others with her instinctive and tacit sense of practice as a teacher; a way of carrying forward her disposition to see potential in kids, and a much more developed sense of herself as an agent of change in the school. She had recognised the value of conversations among staff that acknowledged the emotions involved in teaching. She reported changes in practice in teaching history.

Anne: Increased questioning of the targeted girls, more drama, more student voice, observed the girls, asked other staff [in the school] for opinions, creating learning targets every lesson, raffle for engagement to win chocolate.

These learning targets were about behaviour rather than subject content, a creative way of teaching the pupils the different kinds of engaged behaviour that they wanted to see, focusing on one behaviour at a time and making it a target for the class. These were printed on laminated sheets, and pupils selected one at the start of a lesson. They then discussed as a class how they could demonstrate it, and could win a small prize if they did so.

> *Matt*: One target was 'to respond appropriately to praise'. . . . It even evoked a kind of postmodern ironic response from one of their students, who responded to his teacher's praise by saying, 'Thank you very much, I've learned from that.'

Towards the end of the year, teachers were interviewed about whether the project had been successful. Chris' response was typical.

> *Chris*: I think it has, and for a number of reasons, some direct, others indirect. I think it's made a difference to some targeted girls, at least two in my group of five or six who have really come out of themselves and have become very active members within their group. Another direct result is that it has focused us on looking at observational issues. Therefore, we've devised this series of learning targets that we use in the classroom, that we're going to use in other year groups anyway.

Some of this was shared and adopted by other departments and schools.

> *Chris*: Anne presented a report on the inclusion project to the whole staff at an Inset day earlier this year. We have raised its profile occasionally with a staff meeting and in forums like when she attends the Heads of Department Forum. I've raised it with other schools at my CPD Forum when we were looking at pupil voice. And those schools were very interested in looking at the learning targets.

Matt summed up the development of the group in the following way:

> They keep thinking of different levels of things to add. I think that, I mean I suppose from, I don't know, a theory-generating research point of view, it's a bit tricky because whether it'll end up, as I say, with a formula, I don't know. But I think what it is doing . . ., what, if you like, the business of them being engaged in action research is doing . . . is the best of all possible outcomes: this way of thinking about what's going on is becoming part of how they're doing everything, and they want to do more and more of it. It's not simply about them standing at the front and delivering something as was put in the original paper, blaming kids for not listening, if they weren't. It's about really thinking in as many possible ways and learning from them.

Summarising comments: The history teachers at Main Road began with a real and niggling issue, and kept up their focus on engaging girls as they invented and shared a series of relevant activities, and reflected on their consequences. As a result, and with the support of the EP, they greatly deepened their understanding and appreciation of the girls and what they could do to make lessons more engaging for them. The EP derived pleasure and interest from the role he was able to play, and the impact it made on the teachers.

Targeting boys' disengagement in maths at Main Road (Main Road maths project)

In this other Main Road project, two maths teachers decided early on to target the boys in two Year 9 classes who were on the borderline of achieving a good grade at GCSE. They suspected that these boys in particular had quite negative emotions about maths, and about themselves doing maths. In order to test this, they devised a short questionnaire in which the pupils were invited simply to circle a range of emotions and feelings that applied to them. They could choose from words such as *bored, happy, excited, puzzled, thoughtful, sad, unhappy, friendly, angry, confused, enthusiastic, panicky, pleased, doubtful*. . . .

Throughout the project, the teachers avoided identifying any of the target pupils; they wanted to develop ways of teaching maths that would help all students, as well as making a difference to their target group, without imposing any labels on them. So they had their list, but they gave the questionnaire to all the pupils in their two classes. This was helpful too because they could see whether the target group answered differently from the others – they did, and they were more negative, but it wasn't a big difference. One of the other questions they asked pupils was to rate their enjoyment of teacher-led lessons, group activities and pair work. They found that they felt most negative towards teacher-led activities.

As a result, they set out to change the way they were working with pupils, to involve more group and pair work. This clear focus was significant. They took the curriculum apart, asking themselves how they would normally teach this, and how could they could teach it differently, in line with what they wanted more of. For example, with graphs, they literally made things big, more kinaesthetic. They created A3 laminated graphs, so that they could write on them, and then wipe them clean. Between them they tackled algebra, shape and space, and graphs in this way. The development of resources was significant; they have now made resource-sharing a focus for development in the whole department. The pupils were significantly positive about the changes in their maths lessons, both in questionnaire responses and interviews (see Chapter 3).

The role of the facilitator was partly about keeping things on track, but was more than managerial. Discussions with Matt were very different from their discussions with each other. On their own, they were very task focused, talking and then working out new types of lessons. The EP's questions and enquiries ('Why is that?') dug helpfully and more deeply along a different, more emotional line. It was unusual for these teachers to work in this way with their EP.

The teachers noticed that the project made them think about what they were doing more, and so improved their teaching. The project focused them on the issues of what makes children learn. They recognised that they could have done all this without the project, but also recognised that *most teachers don't*. Set up as a project and with a facilitator, the issue became urgent enough to focus on. Working to a deadline, and having someone ask the right questions at the right time, refocused them on these issues. One of the most surprising outcomes of the project was how much enjoyment the teachers got from talking about and developing their teaching in this way.

Summarising comments: This Main Road project was focused from the start, with just two teachers directly involved, and a clear issue and methodology for addressing it, both in terms of activity and evidence. The teachers developed the new approach from their own practice, but were encouraged to develop further than they had in the past. They themselves were surprised at how much they gained as teachers from seriously addressing what pupils felt about maths, and at how much difference it made to the pupils.

Improving poor language skills at Ysgol y Cwrt (Cwrt cross-subject project)

An overwhelming concern for the school was the poor Welsh-language skills of some pupils. The headteacher decided that a useful project would be to bring together the heads of all humanities departments, working under the leadership of the deputy headteacher to think about ways to address this issue.

A tension that developed in this group was with their relationship with their facilitator. The group were uncertain about the nature of action research, and perceived that the facilitator should provide them with guidance about the process and to act as an expert to advise them about new approaches they could be developing. On her part, the facilitator did not see her role as being an 'expert', wanting to allow teachers to create their own ideas. However, in addition, she did not seem clear about the action research process and this created unnecessary uncertainties for the group.

The choice of the deputy head as the leader had some advantages because she worked hard to support the group. Unfortunately neither she, nor any of the heads of department that made up the group, had very much time to spare for this additional activity, and none was created on a regular basis to support group discussion and preparation.

Despite all these difficulties the teachers eventually decided to implement various visual/pictorial teaching methods (adapted to their subject specialism) to support the engagement of pupils with weak language skills in years 9 and 10. The teachers' evaluation, which relied on subjective impressions, reported that very positive benefits had been observed for pupil motivation, and that as a consequence some staff were experiencing less stress during teaching.

Summarising comments: The project at Ysgol y Cwrt had some beneficial effects across several departments in the development of more accessible resources for pupils struggling with language. However, the lack of discussion and problematising between staff meant that there was no opportunity for a deeper engagement with the issue of language from a pupil perspective.

Tackling disaffection in science at Hightown (Hightown science project)

At the start of this other Hightown project, the new headteacher was focused on addressing falling standards in GCSE results, down from 59 per cent to 47 per cent in 2004, with poor value-added scores. She allocated the project to the relatively low-performing Science Department, and the educational psychologist had initial discussions with the Head of Department and with other staff in a focus group. However, several months later no project had taken shape, and there was a measure of frustration among some staff in the department who saw lots of problems but felt unable to take the initiative to begin addressing them. Other staff appeared rather resigned and apparently disinterested in collaboration.

Eventually, the EP's persistence led the Head of Science to ask John, a young, aspiring and relatively new science teacher, to lead the project. John saw this as an opportunity to influence a group of like-minded staff, and he organised a series of project meetings with five or six staff, who discussed their own practice together, shared ideas, and agreed to focus on 'the first fifteen minutes' of their lessons with 'disaffected' pupils in Year 10. To understand the impact, they used feedback from interviews with a sample of pupils, completed a regular checklist on their lessons, and observed each other's lessons. These were new and engaging activities to most of the staff involved. The project became an opportunity for teachers to learn from each other in non-hierarchical ways; it built on various strengths, such as the scheme of work developed by the Head of Chemistry which specified a range of interesting and relevant starter activities. Lessons improved noticeably as pupils recognised the effort of their teachers to engage them.

The wider impact of this project was not planned, but neither was it accidental. It resulted from three aspects: the significance that it had for participants in terms of the quality of their lessons and relationship with young people; its significance to senior staff in terms of performance of the Science Department, and the work that the EP did to raise the visibility of the project through discussions and letters to staff and school leadership. In addition, throughout the project, John had used performance management meetings to enthuse about the project with the headteacher, who was excited to hear the way the project was helping teachers to address some basic features of more inclusive lessons. Meanwhile, an older and more senior teacher in the department was discovering a renewed interest in the teaching of science, an aspect of her work that had been less of a priority in recent years. Through the meetings, she caught some of the group's enthusiasm and trialled some of the participative approaches that the group was discussing. She invited John to speak about the project to the Assessment for Learning (AfL) group that she led in the school; the headteacher later asked him to speak to the whole staff at an Inset day in June 2006. He presented the project enthusiastically but in a very down-to-earth way: 'It's not rocket science' . . . and earned an enthusiastic round of applause from the staff. A large teaching and learning group was set up to further embed the projects' approaches across the school, with most of the young staff attending. A staffroom whiteboard was installed to share ideas about teaching and learning, and the tone of staffroom conversations appeared to shift towards a more problem-solving orientation.

Summarising comments: The Hightown project highlights the issues of timeliness and connection, critical to the meaningfulness of the project in a large and relatively stuck department. Action research had a powerful effect on teachers in the department, making the dominant culture much more participative and positive in approach. Teachers no longer felt 'excluded' but were able to take back the initiative and to think and work more positively with their pupils.

Assisting pupils with weak language skills at Bont (Bont RE project)

Ysgol y Bont is a bilingual but mainly Welsh-medium secondary comprehensive school of approximately 900 pupils located in a rural village in West Wales. It accepts all children from its community, and although all those arriving from local feeder primary schools will have been educated through the medium of Welsh, the level of pupil fluency is variable owing to factors such as the first language of the home. About 8 per cent of pupils receive free school meals, less than 1 per cent are from ethnic minority backgrounds and 11 per cent are on the special needs register.

The teachers who participated in the school project were selected by the headteacher. The small RE department of three teachers was chosen. All participated initially but after a time one dropped out, leaving a group of two. This group size was too small to easily provide a varied range of opinions to stimulate discussion. The position of one group member was dominant due to her seniority as Head of Department, her greater experience and her forceful leadership, so this did not facilitate full and frank discussions between her and her more junior colleague. The Head of Department was unimpressed by action research from the outset; she wanted to move quickly in order to save time, and to 'fast forward' through the stage of reflection to get down, as soon as possible, to practical action in the classroom. In recognising this situation, the facilitator was anxious to help the teachers to benefit from the opportunities for reflection but observed that once the group 'set up the project, they wanted to forget all about the process'.

As a result, a decision was briskly taken by the teachers to focus the project on providing better support for pupils with weak language skills. The additional support of vocabulary mats and dictionaries was provided to pupils in years 7, 8 and 9 in their RE lessons. No new evaluation methods were developed or implemented. At the end of the project the teachers observed that the boys (who had been identified as having on the whole poorer language skills) were answering many more questions, and one teacher considered that their marks had improved.

The teachers viewed the impact of the project on themselves as bringing more work to prepare but providing no additional time to do so. Since it was considered that free time needs to be found to meet the demands of action research, they regarded traditional INSET as more effective.

Summarising comments: The dominant sense at Bont was of teachers working in a mode typical of the pressurised environment of many schools. The problem was defined on the basis of teachers' existing experience and assumptions – pupils have poor vocabulary, dictionaries might help – and there was little time or impulse to reflect more deeply than this.

Adapting to different learning styles in Ysgol y Neuadd (Neuadd cross-subject project)

A large group of six teachers from a very diverse range of departments volunteered for this project, stimulated by the account of the other Neuadd project related at a staff meeting. This very large and varied group presented a challenge to the facilitator. Not all members were present at most meetings, so it became difficult to move forward the discussion with full agreement and ownership. The diversity of subject specialisms represented, although providing a rich vein of experience for discussion, made it more difficult to agree how to move forward with a shared focus. The facilitator felt some momentum was lost over the summer vacation period, and the group members expressed concerns that the facilitation style had not helped teaches to focus on a topic once one had emerged. In Phase II the facilitators were provided with a toolkit by the University but some still continued to experience difficulties with the role.

After an often useful but prolonged period of discussion, the group decided to develop teaching techniques that would enable them to provide for a wider range of learning styles among their pupils. The trialling of assessment techniques for learning styles, and the development of the use of different teaching approaches (e.g. learner activities that use the kinaesthetic sense), led to a lot of useful questioning and thinking by individual teachers and within the collaborative group about the value of learning styles research.

Despite the uneven progress of the project many of the group reported a strong appreciation of the opportunities for collaboration, particularly across departments.

After the conclusion of both phases, the headteacher reflected positively on the value of action research, 'It has really helped us to be talking about the nuts and bolts of teaching and learning, and pupil learning.'

Summarising comments: At Ysgol y Neuadd, learning styles provided a focus for discussion and eventually trialling of various activities, not joint but aligned, which made possible some valuable conversations among teachers, questioning and deepening their understanding of differences between pupils.

Drawing out themes

Reflecting on the project work in schools as it was proceeding, we aimed to identify features of those projects that were having a significant impact on classrooms and teachers, and to check out whether these features distinguished projects from those having apparently less impact. We introduce three key issues here; further aspects such as facilitation will be considered more fully in Chapters 4 and 5.

The first key issue was **collaboration** between teachers. Drawing on each other's insights and ideas of others and making changes in practice would be impossible for one person to sustain on their own. Collaboration also involves sharing the risks, and encouraging each other. Furthermore, working with pupils as well as staff is a powerful source of challenging and fruitful ideas for development, and potentially a great source of continuing energy.

Some of the groups that started with actions collaborated in a way that involved significant discussions and greater understanding of underlying issues. For example, the teachers involved at Ysgol y Neuadd drew together around a particular action to improve engagement in learning – experimenting with pupil whiteboards. In starting to discuss impact, they developed their understanding of what pupil engagement looks and feels like in practice, as well as their classroom repertoires. These actions led the teachers to reflect further on key educational ideas. Collaboration here was not simply about working alongside each other; instead, it involved teachers discussing the rationale for particular action and evidence for its impact. Critical engagement within the group was necessary, rather than simply group membership. In this sense, collaboration was significant to the extent that it built on the different perspectives of those involved, and involved them in understanding more about each other's position.

A similar process of collaboration was apparent at Ysgol y Pentre, where teachers were aiming to use peer mentoring to create more useful and sustainable relationships between pupils of different ages in the school. They came to this with different priorities, with the head of the sixth form, for example, more interested than others in what older pupils might gain from the experience of mentoring. The group demonstrated that older peers could provide valuable support to pupils at risk of failure. In doing so, they strengthened their contribution to the school as a group that cared about and worked for these things. They were aided in this by the active support and encouragement of the facilitator, and by combining their individual strengths as a team. As a result, the headteacher learned something about the value of giving teachers some autonomy over a project of their own.

By comparison, there was little need for such critical collaboration on the project at Ysgol y Cwrt. The learning resource focus of the teachers' work with coloured filters was one that teachers were able to explore without much assistance, and relatively unproblematically, because they already had a shared understanding. Although they strengthened their sense of working together in the process, there was little need for collaboration which involved discussing rationale for action challenging some of their assumptions and contributing to a more subtle approach towards adapting resources. However, collaboration occurring among staff bringing the different perspectives of learning support and a subject specialism provided new opportunities for understanding an issue in the round.

The ambitious attempt at Hightown to pilot a new reward system worked well owing to the combination of energetic and committed form tutors, the involvement of a member of senior staff to ensure resourcing, and the facilitator's ability to assist reflection and decision-making based on evidence from young people.

The second key issue that we identified was **ownership**: teachers who owned an issue and process did so in terms that were meaningful to them at that time. They put energy into thinking through the consequences for themselves and their practice; and they were prepared to take some risks in trying to resolve the issue. Where a group owned the issue, they created a space together to follow it through. Where other conditions allowed, they were able to persuade others in school of the wider significance of their work. Thus, for example, the project at Ysgol y Parc started with analysis by teachers and facilitator around pupil disengagement, and then the selection of teaching approaches that might be more motivating for pupils. For the teachers concerned, the significant outcome was in terms of positive relationships with pupils. However, as in several other projects, these changes were very localised, with the project remaining disconnected from the wider school and from making a wider impact. At Main Road, ownership of the issue was even stronger for the history teachers: they began with a real and niggling issue, and kept up their focus on engaging girls as they invented and shared a series of relevant activities, and reflected on their consequences. As a result, and with the facilitation of the EP, they greatly deepened their understanding and appreciation of these pupils and what they could do to make lessons more engaging for them. The EP also derived pleasure and interest from the role he was able to play, and the impact it made on the teachers.

The maths project at Main Road was also focused from the start, with the two teachers directly involved having an issue they wanted to address and a methodology for addressing it, both in terms of activity and evidence. They developed the new approach from their own practice, but were engaged enough with the process to develop much further than they had in the past. As a consequence, they themselves were surprised at how much they gained as teachers from seriously addressing what pupils felt about maths, and at how much difference it made to the pupils. By comparison, in the large and relatively stuck Hightown Science Department, the development of ownership and meaning to the project had to wait until connections were made and the opportunity was timely. It was only then that action research began to have a powerful effect on the teachers in the department, shifting the dominant culture to a more participative and positive orientation. Teachers felt less 'excluded', able to take back the initiative and to think and work more positively with their pupils. At Ysgol y Neuadd, learning styles was an issue that provided a focus for discussion and eventually trialling of various activities, aligned rather than joint, and this made possible some valuable conversations between teachers, questioning and deepening their understanding of differences between pupils.

At Ysgol y Cwrt, the group that focused on improving poor language skills had much weaker group ownership of the issues. The project had some beneficial effects across several departments through the development of more accessible resources for pupils struggling with language. However, the lack of discussion and problematising by staff created no opportunity for a deeper engagement with the issue of language from a pupil perspective. The dominant sense at Ysgol y Bont was of teachers working in a mode typical of the pressurised environment of many schools. Teachers defined the problem on the basis of their existing experience and assumptions – pupils have poor vocabulary, dictionaries might help – and there was little time or impulse to reflect more deeply than this – this was not a group grappling with an issue that they considered significant to them.

The third key issue identified was that of **interaction with evidence**. When teachers planned to find out what difference they were making, it made them more alert to the process they were involved in. They talked more about what they noticed, and checked it out with each other. They searched out reasons for what was happening, and all this helped them to develop their understanding, and to refine what they were doing. This was not creating data for the sake of it – it was purposeful, and it often had valuable unintended consequences.

To provide a more detailed view, the final column in Table 3.2 is a summary of the impact on teachers' learning of interaction with evidence. The impact of the projects on pupils is the subject of the following chapter. Here the focus is on the effect of teachers reflecting on data in terms of their own understanding and commitment to change.

The impact of data falls into three groups. In those projects where little data were generated by teachers, the impact of their subjective impressions on their thinking was minimal. They tended to see what they expected to see, and so there was little opportunity for challenge. This is not surprising, given the way human beings tend to perceive the world; Bertrand Russell expressed it succinctly in the following way:

> If a man is offered a fact which goes against his instincts, he will scrutinize it closely, and unless the evidence is overwhelming, he will refuse to believe it. If, on the other hand, he is offered something which affords a reason for acting in accordance with his instincts, he will accept it even on the slenderest evidence.
>
> (Russell 1918; http://www.solstice.us/russell/proposed.html)

In contrast, there were projects where as teachers worked out a way of measuring or assessing the impact of their actions, they deepened their understanding of classroom processes together. Here it was not so much the data generated that had an impact as the thinking that went into what data to generate and how. This discussion was an element in many

Table 3.2 The impact on teachers' learning of interaction with evidence

School project	Issue addressed	Pedagogical action	Impact of data
Bont RE	Welsh-language skills	Learning resource development	Confirmatory evidence of greater pupil involvement did not challenge teachers' assumptions
Cwrt cross-subject	Welsh-language skills	Teaching approaches	Informal data provided little challenge to teachers' assumptions
Cwrt SEN	Reading ability	Learning resource development	Results confounded teachers' assumptions and provoked thinking
Hightown pastoral	Pupil reward scheme	Institutional organisation	Pupil perspectives led to better understanding of what motivated pupils. Evidence of positive impact on discipline was consolidating of position
Hightown science	Disaffection in science	Teaching approaches	Peer observation, teacher checklist and pupil feedback all invigorated teachers' discussion and thinking
Main Road history	Girls' underachievement	Teaching approaches	Pupil feedback and teacher observation of pupils invigorated teachers' thinking
Main Road maths	Boys' disaffection	Learning resource development	Pupil questionnaire and feedback on their learning was powerful confirmatory evidence for teachers
Neuadd cross-subject	Diverse learning styles	Teaching approaches	Results confounded teachers' assumptions and provoked thinking
Neuadd Welsh	Pupil participation	Teaching approaches	Teachers' discussion of pupil engagement was greatly deepened by the attempt to measure it
Parc science	Pupil motivation	Teaching approaches	Teachers realised the value of pupil feedback
Pentre pastoral	Peer mentoring	Institutional organisation	Somewhat contradictory evidence led teachers to a better understanding of complexity

projects, and fits with the notion of the theory of change: deciding on how to assess impact entails thinking as clearly as possible about what is likely to change, and how, as a result of the actions taken.

Finally, in projects in which teachers reflected on data generated through interviews and questionnaires with pupils, and through observation of pupils in lessons, their assumptions were often confounded in a way that stimulated their thinking.

We will return to each of these three key issues in the next chapter. First, though, we compare projects in terms of the types of actions that were taken by teachers.

The actions that teachers took

As we have mentioned, there was a common outline for the involvement of schools in Prosiect Dysgu Cydradd, and so it was fascinating to observe the range of actions that teachers chose to engage in. The **pedagogical actions** that teachers developed may be categorised into three groups: teaching approaches, learning resources and institutional organisation (see Table 3.2). Some actions had elements of two or more of these, but nevertheless the emphasis in each is clear.

- *Learning resource development* focused on new resources for pupils: coloured filters to aid reading; big maths; dictionaries and vocabulary mats. Significantly, the engagement of teachers in projects in this group varied enormously, and the comparison between them demonstrates that the production or adoption of new learning resources in itself is not at all sufficient for the development of more inclusive practice.
- *Teaching approaches* represented the most direct form of change, made by teachers into the way they practised in their classrooms. These included a routine and structured start to lessons, the use of pupil whiteboards and pupil feedback on lessons. Such a list of teacher activities looks unremarkable. Many teachers may say 'we do those things already'. While this is no doubt true, the main point here is that these are actions which have been considered, tried out, and then become an established part of teachers' practice, appropriate to their particular context, in a context where they had previously not been used.
- *Institutional organisation* was addressed in terms of reward schemes and peer mentoring. Aiming for institutional change probably represents the most ambitious type of action in relation to an action

research approach. Interestingly, both of these projects were carried out by pastoral teams aiming to develop better school systems for support and motivation of pupils, while only one of them had the unequivocal support of senior management (Main Road pastoral). The Pentre pastoral project shows how a group of teachers can create new institutional processes which are well integrated into existing systems and draw on underused strengths.

In each school project, the significance of the pedagogical action taken cannot be understood separately from the processes which surrounded that action. The projects focusing on the development of learning resources varied most widely in terms of impact, probably because the adoption of new resources is possible without any significant effort from teachers to reconsider their practice. The prime case here was the Bont RE project, where busy teachers assumed that the introduction of dictionaries and vocabulary mats constituted an adequate response to pupils' language issues. This project engaged teachers only marginally in considering pupils' experience of lessons. This compares strongly with another learning resource development project, Main Road maths, where the teachers gained considerable professional confidence around their adaptation of pupil resources, as a result of their enquiry, reflection and discussion of impact.

Around the three key themes already identified, of collaboration, ownership and interaction with evidence, other significant elements of process emerge, along with features of context which support these processes. It is important not to overlook the contribution of individuals to these projects, drawing on their diverse experience. Individuals have expert skills and diverse experiences of teaching and learning and research. For example, in Hightown science, one teacher had great skill in constructing imaginative schemes of work; in Main Road maths, one teacher had a lot of experience with visual aids. They differed in terms of determination to make something happen: for instance, the Cwrt SEN project thrived on the basis of the infectious interest of one teacher in the application of technology to the reading process. This determination is one of leadership; some projects depended largely on the leadership offered by one individual, such as in Hightown science and the Pentre pastoral project, whereas in others, various individuals combined to lead the project together, as in the Main Road history project. As a general rule, the leadership of projects emerged rather than being agreed from the start – which suggests that leadership is not something to view as a precondition which must be established in advance, although there does need to be an acknowledgement of the legitimacy of leadership by one or more of a group as it emerges.

Projects were affected too by the amount of time made available for them, and by the capacity of the facilitator to support, sustain and encourage development. For example, in the Parc science project, the facilitator played a central role in introducing ideas in a timely way. As indicated, these aspects will be considered more fully in the following chapters. In terms of sustainability of project outcomes in the context of complex school organisations, another vital area was the linking of projects to the wider school context, often through links with specific institutional processes such as teacher appraisal, promotion, or the development of AfL across the school.

Conclusion

It is a challenge to convey briefly in writing the nature and detail of teacher action research in these eleven projects. Reviewing this chapter, the risk of misreading the significance of these projects within these schools is apparent. These were busy secondary schools, with teachers attending to the many competing demands on their time and energy. The stories we have presented are situated in the middle of all that activity, and represent how teachers responded to and built on an opportunity to focus together on an issue of particular importance to them, identifying a strand of activity which they thought likely to influence pupils' engagement in learning. We have identified three aspects of this process which when attended to appeared to make the process more fulfilling and useful to teachers, and considered the effect on teachers and pupils of different types of pedagogic action. In the next chapter, we focus further on the factors which helped and hindered teachers' engagement.

Chapter 4

What helped teachers

The case studies we described in the previous chapter are examples of teachers working together within the complex social system of their schools to develop more inclusive practice. We used the case studies to begin to identify key elements of more engaging processes for teachers. In this chapter, we draw on further data from case studies and make more use of cross-comparison between case studies to create a framework of themes which facilitate to serve the engagement of teachers, and those which hinder it.

The case studies in the previous chapter have told the stories of the eleven teacher projects, of teachers working together within the complex social system of their schools to achieve changes in their practice. They are narratives of effort, endeavour and for most groups some success. However, as we have seen, although most projects resulted in some useful outcomes, the trajectories of the projects varied greatly, as did teachers' experience of involvement in those projects. In some schools, there is every likelihood that the processes developed will continue to be used and to be useful in bringing about further change. In other schools, it appears that the end of the project also marked the end of such a process of engagement by teachers.

The implication of this is the need to build up practices in schools which contribute to that engagement by teachers, out of which can come teacher identities of agency, and a hopeful, practice-oriented discourse of inclusion. This is not something that can be established at a stroke; engagement *emerges* along with a sense of agency, and the opportunity to make meaning together. We will be arguing that there is no alternative path to the development of meaningful inclusion than through this emergent process of teacher engagement. Emerging meaning and sense-making is at the heart of the construction of an increasingly principled position, a sense of self-efficacy as a teacher. That implies a language of engagement – expressing what pupils value; what teachers value; what teachers want to be for their pupils (identities), and what teachers are trying to create and move towards (meaningful contexts; vivid examples; quality of relationship).

In this chapter we compare and contrast cases to identify, among the diversity of experience that they represent, the elements that are critical to the effective engagement of teachers. This is the focus of our first research question: What factors relating to teachers and their learning environment facilitate or hinder schools/teachers from engaging in collaborative action research with the aim of developing inclusion? As identified in Chapter 3, three key issues stand out in successful action research for inclusion: *collaboration, ownership* and *interaction with evidence*. We explore these issues further, examining why they are meaningful for teachers, and how they link to other significant aspects of life in schools, such as pace of change, styles of leadership and approaches to performance management. In doing so, we begin to identify how a context for inclusion can develop through teachers' engagement in pedagogical actions and processes, with emphasis on some features of context which can be changed. We conclude the chapter by bringing together these ideas in a framework for analysing and guiding collaborative action research for inclusion.

We begin by identifying some features of the context in which teachers work which become apparent through the comparison of the different cases.

Similarities and differences in teachers' contexts

The features of the development process valued by teachers were very much linked to the contexts in which they found themselves, and we first summarise some of the similarities and differences in these contexts. Contextual similarities across schools included teachers' own practice and their practical knowledge of inclusion and action research. First, for example, and very common among all groups, was the sense of uncertainty around the *practicalities of inclusion*. Inclusion was a well-known concept to teachers, whose definitions accorded well with those of the researchers and project leaders.

Nearly all teachers knew enough about inclusion to define it readily, for instance, in questionnaire responses (Bont RE, Cwrt cross-subject and SEN, Neuadd Welsh and cross-subject, Parc science, Pentre pastoral, Hightown science and pastoral, Main Road history and maths), Teachers talked about inclusion as a right for all pupils, in a way typified by the following definitions:

'[A]llowing all students to access the curriculum at a level suitable for them; the access must be real in lessons, not just on paper' (teacher, Hightown science)

'[I]nclusion means involving and engaging all (or vast majority) of students in a meaningful and relevant curriculum. However this may involve considerably differing curricula for different students' (teacher, Hightown science).

For many teachers though, definitions and rhetoric about inclusion were better developed than the practice. Inclusion for many was often experienced as difficult to implement (Bont RE, Cwrt cross-subject and SEN, Parc science, Neuadd Welsh and cross-subject). This level of uncertainty was reflected in the large number of teachers who later said that engaging in the project had changed the way they thought about inclusion, realising, for instance, that 'inclusion is everyone not just those with educational, behavioural, learning difficulties'.

The project made a difference in practice, for example, in helping 'to provide some further strategies to encourage higher achievement . . . [and] made me realise that inclusion is a "whole class" issue, and not just related to SEN or EBD' (teacher at Main Road).

Second, *action research* was an unfamiliar process, and not one clearly understood by most teachers (Cwrt cross-subject and SEN, Neuadd Welsh and cross-subject, Bont RE, Pentre pastoral). It was often initially perceived and experienced as vague and open-ended (Cwrt cross-subject, Bont RE) but was seen to be accessible when it was understood in context (Main Road history and maths, Parc science). Unsurprisingly therefore, teachers valued guidance on and facilitation of the process of action research (Parc science, Pentre pastoral), but this had to be guidance appropriate to the group of teachers and to their current context. Where this didn't happen effectively, teachers bypassed reflection and 'fast forwarded' towards action (Bont RE, Cwrt cross-subject) or experienced a lack of direction (Cwrt cross-subject) and loss of momentum (Neuadd Welsh and cross-subject).

These two aspects of context then were common to most schools. In addition, in terms of the project, the starting point in all schools was similar. The previous chapter outlined the clear but limited guidance and structure that was offered: how schools were invited to identify a group of teachers and a focus for action research relating to pupils' engagement in their learning, and then to complete a project within two terms, with the help of the educational psychologist.

However, there were of course considerable differences in the school contexts in which the project was realised. The case studies demonstrate how the common project starting point led to a diversity of approaches, groups and intentions. This diversity was evident in the case studies in terms of *focus*: groups of teachers looked at the impact of changes in, for example, lesson structures, getting feedback from pupils, and agreeing group targets with pupils; and the groups of relatively disengaged pupils they focused on included boys, girls, particular year groups, and particularly underachieving individuals. The *speed of focusing* varied tremendously: in some schools an initial starting point quickly opened up teachers' individual and shared assumptions about the pupils concerned, and led to effective and agreed group action (Main Road history, Parc science, Pentre pastoral). Others spent a long time feeling uncertain about what to focus on, and how, and also on settling into agreed roles for the duration of the project (Neuadd Welsh); and in one case this seemed to link to the different subject areas involved, so that members worked to their own agendas but met to discuss them every so often (Cwrt cross-subject). Two other groups struggled like this initially, until in various ways an individual member took the initiative and drove the process forward to a useful conclusion (Hightown science and pastoral). One group adopted a no-nonsense approach by defining a problem and implementing a possible solution, spending little time in the process on exploring issues or evaluating the impact of their actions (Bont RE). Another group involved a support assistant in an innovative way, driven forward by a plan and the enthusiasm of one member, supported by the others (Cwrt SEN). A pair of teachers working together in one case made considerable progress with a highly focused action, maintaining a clear sense of direction and commitment to the development they envisaged together (Main Road maths).

This variation reflects the different responses of the teachers, the facilitator and the school to the challenges that developing inclusion through action research present to the individual professional and to the school. Taking account of these different responses is our starting point for understanding the features of context and process in which those challenges can be better met.

The case studies provide the opportunity to distinguish features of the development process and context which were important to teachers: the chance to engage critically; to work collaboratively with colleagues; to make the project their own; and to pay close attention to what was going on in their classroom, especially around pupil involvement.

We have discussed the way in which action research projects that began with a common structure resulted in quite different experiences for the teachers involved – and sometimes in different experiences for teachers in the same school. This range of recorded experience, extending from valued opportunities to frustrations and challenges, is a valuable resource for investigating how to engage teachers. Just what was it that made the difference? What has been learnt about engaging teachers with the issue of inclusion?

In the remainder of this chapter we distinguish between three areas of response to this question. In all cases it is a question of organisation, structure and relationships. Effectively engaging teachers is first about the teacher group, because teaching is a social activity, and the norms of daily practice are made, sustained and shifted by groups of colleagues. Second, it depends on the system of the school, because so many of the constraints on practice, and opportunities for its development, are determined by the division of labour and the rules for doing things that are characteristic of the school as a whole. Third, we have learnt about the challenges and possibilities for sustaining a change in culture which encourages more autonomous development by teachers. We begin with the development of a space in which teachers can work together.

Creating and structuring a space for teachers' engagement

As we have seen in the preceding section, many teachers in the case studies valued the opportunity that the action research process offered of a respite from the 'everydayness' of teaching, and the chance for sustained conversations and enquiry focusing on a shared problem. But it was also clear that simply having space to discuss, reflect and decide on priorities for action is not in itself necessarily of value to teachers. Such space is sometimes regarded as wasteful, given the many daily demands on teachers. In what follows, we revisit the framework established in the previous chapter, looking particularly at the issues of ownership, collaboration and interaction with evidence, to see what they meant in terms of teachers' experience in their projects.

Ownership

A vital stage in all projects was the negotiation of an issue that was relevant and meaningful to the staff involved. The groups of teachers who most fully engaged in an action research project had an opportunity to decide their specific focus of action for themselves (Parc science, Pentre pastoral, Main Road history and maths, Hightown science and pastoral). Such ownership appears to be a necessary condition, such that the project offered a route beyond broad definitions of inclusion. Many teachers who reflected in questionnaires and interviews on the value of the process identified the increase in motivation it gave them to engage again with the details of their practice, in a way which led them towards more inclusive thinking and practice.

'I really enjoyed it – it gave me a chance to rethink my own teaching' (teacher, Main Road history)

'It was much easier to know what pupils had understood and adjust teaching accordingly' (teacher, Neuadd Welsh).

Ownership of process mattered far more to teachers than strict adherence to a process of research, which has implications for facilitators. An important tool for facilitators in constructing ownership proved to be a teacher focus group, used to explore practitioners' *theories of change* and the way they saw things (Connell and Kubisch 1998). The facilitator invited teachers to consider a group of pupils whom they felt were disengaged in lessons, reflect on the nature of their concerns about those pupils, and then identify a range of strategies that might influence that situation. This focus group discussion provided a starting point from which the group and facilitator could decide on actions and ways of evaluating their effect.

Finding a socially meaningful shared focus was not always straightforward, but it made a huge difference to a project.

'When we were successful in our bid to the senior management to be involved in this project, we decided to limit initial involvement to the two more experienced teachers in the department – one a teacher for twelve years, the other a teacher for seven years who is also head of department. For both of us, this became a significant opportunity for professional development. After several years working in the same school, it was good to have the chance to extend ourselves, stand back a bit and focus in a different way on the basics of what it is to teach maths well. The work we did with University of Manchester is the sort of thing we do anyway, but it was good to be encouraged to focus more time on it and to see it as development work that could benefit us as teachers, the department, and the school as a whole' (teacher, Main Road maths).

Ownership by teachers meant that projects were more likely to be timely and connected to the needs that teachers themselves perceived. This had implications for the language with which projects were framed – and it is important to be aware of this aspect, since it runs counter to much of the received wisdom about inclusive practice. In short, in the most effective projects the language was that of the teachers themselves, and often this was not the 'language of inclusion'. For example, the language of the person who coordinated the science project at Hightown:

'10B2 is the more notorious of all the classes . . . somebody christened them "nice but dim, bright but grim". I think there's an issue . . . if we can nail them we can sort the others as well . . . so we're thinking if we can get order and sense to the first fifteen minutes . . . then they might get switched on.'

These are the words of a teacher speaking to colleagues in terms they will relate to, communicated in terms very judgemental of this class. The problem is defined as located with the pupils, some of whom are seen to lack intelligence, others lacking manners and appropriate control over their behaviour. There are no overtones of inclusion-speak here; it sounds blunt, forthright and unreflective. But it is this very language that brought colleagues into the project, to see that there was something there for them. At the same time, there is a way forward being proposed: that teachers take responsibility for making the start of lessons sensible and orderly. Through further discussion within the group and with the EP, it was relatively straightforward to make the actions proposed go further, towards creating interesting, motivating starts to lessons. The result was a project which (in the words of the EP) had

'left its mark – there is now a working group set up in school looking at teaching and learning. The staffroom whiteboard is being used as a reminder to staff about getting a good start – it had changed since my last visit. Whiteboard reminder today had the following prompts: "meet, seat 'n' greet; starter activity; lesson objectives; take register at appropriate time". In addition, there were nine examples of starter activities on an A4 sheet contributed by different teachers across the curriculum' (EP, Hightown).

Where, in contrast, teacher involvement or their focus was imposed by others, for example, through departmental hierarchies and by senior management, teachers' commitment to the project was much less evident (Bont RE, Neuadd Welsh), though the words paid lip-service to inclusion.

However, even where ownership was implicitly recognised as important to the process, there were differences. The evidence of the case studies suggests that ownership is significant throughout the process, but that it entails different issues at different points. Initially, ownership is about striking a balance between allowing real issues to emerge, and establishing a focus within a reasonable time. On the one hand, as several case studies demonstrate, teachers cannot immediately articulate the issues they want to focus on (Main Road history, Pentre pastoral). Without the freedom to develop ideas, to think things through and to try things out, they are unlikely to move to a more critical position in relation to their practice, and so the possibilities for change remain limited. Some of the teachers who most valued the opportunity stressed the need to be hands-on as part of the development process. They talked of 'the chance to focus . . . doing is much better than listening. Action research embeds effectively, as does any hands-on activity' (Main Road history). On the other hand, freedom without guidance is debilitating. Several groups struggled for too long to clarify their direction, and as a result lost momentum and focus, and any sense of directing their own development.

From another perspective, ownership of a project can only develop where at least some teachers are keen to grasp the opportunity for taking action according to their own appraisal of a situation, as opposed to implementing policy and procedures decided by others. In some case studies, such readiness was linked to dissatisfaction with the predominant model of change in the institution (Pentre pastoral) and there was a feeling that the project was an opportunity to address important issues that would otherwise be ignored. In others, teachers were willing to develop and try out their own ideas in the absence of any strong steer from managers or others (Neuadd Welsh, Main Road history). There were several different reasons for this, including their own professional ambition, their imaginative sense of how things might be better, and their clarity about their own efficacy in addressing classroom issues.

Later, in order to maintain the momentum of a project, ownership has to be understood in terms of who within the group has responsibility for decisions; how tasks are allocated to individuals, and how difficulties are addressed. All projects relied on the willingness of at least some teachers to take responsibility for the purposeful use of available time, and for coordination among team members. In several projects, a key individual became important at this stage, offering energy and commitment to a group that might otherwise have run out of steam (Hightown science), and cutting through an excess of possibilities to help the group towards a manageable shared purpose (Cwrt SEN). Such a person is not necessarily acting as the formal project leader, but in taking responsibility for others' learning is implicitly accepting a management role in the group. Sometimes, such roles overlap with those of the facilitator; leadership and facilitation is a subject for further discussion in a later chapter. In summary: effective group leadership is important, and was found to be most effective when this leadership emerged through the opportunities presented by the process.

Looking across the projects, it is evident that the significant ownership by less engaged teachers often comes about because of colleagues who know them and are in a position to encourage their involvement. Ownership is partly about a freedom to make choices and to experiment with possibilities, but not in isolation. Autonomy becomes real in a particular context through the interaction with other teachers. Several cases demonstrate the significance of recognition by engaged teachers of how other colleagues are placed and can become involved. For example, the Hightown science project was meaningful to both an experienced senior teacher and to a recently newly qualified teacher, among others; this was the result of the work done by the eventual project leader in tailoring the purpose of the project to the needs of the individuals involved, and in helping them to see the value of putting their energy into it, despite other agendas. A similar subtle ownership is evident in Parc science, where the EP played this communicative role. Ownership is not accidental; it is initially achieved through offering teachers real choice, and then it has to be continually constructed and maintained in a particular context. When it is, it becomes a site of expansive learning, where issues of significance are dealt with.

Collaboration

All the cases described in the previous chapter suggest that outcomes of projects depend partly on the quality of collaboration between them. Collaboration begins with the willingness and ability of individuals to work together with colleagues. One of the most emotive and striking messages that came from engagement with teachers in the research was that more than a small minority of them felt *themselves* to be alienated and excluded from school processes. This was unexpected – it appeared that in unpacking the notion of inclusion for pupils, their own personal feelings of being marginalised came to the surface. In some cases it seemed to be that their voice had not been listened to and that they did not feel that they had any influence over policy and strategy. Sometimes teachers made a direct link to the issue of inclusion.

> 'Including teachers is the first thing. Teachers can feel excluded from what is going on in what is changing in schools. How can you change what is happening without getting the staff involved? All too easily, current teachers feel that they are out of it. There are different ways of excluding teachers – some didn't get included in the project, who wanted to be included' (teachers' focus group, Hightown science and Main Road history)

> 'Schools should look after teachers better. To keep them feeling good about themselves, so that they can feel good about the kids. Not piling on the pressure constantly' (teachers' focus group, Parc science).

Individual teachers who felt excluded – not necessarily by the design of others in the school, but as an unintended consequence of structures – found it initially difficult to be enthusiastic about this sort of development. Some either never got involved or soon dropped out. However, others discovered that the project provided an alternative to their habitual disengagement, and found themselves working with colleagues in new ways. Sometimes this was a surprise for everyone, as where in Hightown science, one relatively senior and experienced teacher with wider school responsibilities enthusiastically described new possibilities of re-engaging with the Science Department, and learning from younger colleagues:

> 'This is the Year 11 class. You know, they are liable to . . . you put a test in front of them and "we haven't done that", that sort of

reaction that you get from them. So, that's the issue I have with this group; so in discussions with [teacher's name] and watching something that he had done, we've set them the task in two lessons that they have been assigned a little section of the syllabus and they've got to teach it. . . . This was our first hour. The second hour they've got to produce a handout, an audiovisual, and a talk that's got to last no less than five minutes and no more than ten minutes. . . . They all got straight into it and they responded and engaged with it' (teacher, Hightown science).

For this senior teacher, her description here demonstrates a dramatic change of orientation towards science teachinng. It represented her re-engagement and responsibility for leading the learning of her science classes.

In other schools there were groups of teachers who had become relatively marginalised through the contradictions of current leadership priorities and historical structures. In Pentre pastoral, such a group of teachers who felt disregarded by the school leadership viewed the project as a source of strength to them in developing an imaginative and practical intervention to bring a vital missing dimension back to the school community. The project gained a micro-political significance, and helped those teachers to release energy productively when they had previously felt only aggrieved.

Only very few groups started confidently with a discussion of their educational values, or used such discussion as a collaborative starting point (Howes and Fox 2006). This links to the point made in the last section about ownership of the process depending on teachers initially using their own language and way of framing the issue, rather than adopting a language of inclusion which initially has little meaning for them. Most groups of teachers discussing the challenges they faced began by identifying causes external to themselves (e.g. Bont RE, Cwrt cross-subject) before considering actions they could take. But evidence suggests that a collaborative space can be created, even where teachers are constrained by other agendas (e.g. Main Road history and maths, Pentre pastoral). A group can be helped towards a shared focus, either through early joint activity (Neuadd cross-subject, Parc science), or through more extended initial reflection (Hightown science, Main Road history).

It was not only relatively marginalised teachers who gained from the project. This Head of Department is frank about her initial focus and the unlooked-for impact on her own teaching:

'It has given me something to think about in class. I think I was coming from a project area point of view of like the leader of the department rather than the history teacher. . . . I think, you know, along the way I must have thought, "oh yeah, it's been really good for my teaching", which nowadays, isn't as much of a focus as perhaps it should be' (Head of History at Main Road).

Although collaboration took many forms in different projects, teachers' everyday talk was always an important part of the process of change. Again and again, teachers mentioned the value of talking to each other. They recognised that, crucially, 'we have talked to each other more about teaching and learning, not just about the administrative questions' (teacher, Main Road history). The project opened up conversations about pedagogy, as explained by teachers from Neuadd cross-subject during a project meeting:

T2: We've talked about teaching and learning styles, which we wouldn't.

T1: Yeah, we wouldn't.

I: What would you normally be talking about, then, with other teachers?

T2: About the weather, or the rugby, or . . .

T1: Or you might say, 'Oh, you know, how's this child doing? They're really naughty for me.' 'Oh, they're really naughty for me too.'

I: Yeah, yeah.

T1: But you wouldn't then go into, 'What teaching style do you implement in order to, you know . . .'

I: OK.

T1: It's not about application. It's almost as if it's, what's the word for it, when you don't talk about it?

I: Taboo?

T2: Yeah. Which is bizarre, isn't it, really?

I: What, not to talk about how you teach?

T1: Yes.

T2: Yes, I suppose.

These teachers valued a process that was clearly about application of principles in their daily practice. Developments took place which made teaching 'less stressful' (teacher, Cwrt cross-subject) owing to a more relaxed approach to teaching, and better relationships with students. Collaboration that involved sharing the detail of practice led to 'improvements in the teaching environment'. Meetings of a group of science teachers, for example, were:

> 'a great source of just little ideas, just inspiration, just small snippets of ideas to just go and, you know, to go and do with a particular class. . . . [Such as] just a little game that, you know, to end a lesson, or to get engaged, to hook them back in and it's just a simple word game. . . . Because one of the things, sometimes I think "I haven't managed it", I haven't injected any fun at all, but that was one of the things that they were saying they wanted a bit more fun' (teacher, Hightown science).

Collaborating with colleagues in this way led many teachers to change their practical understanding of inclusion: 'I now realise how important it is to understand how each individual within the lesson learns' (teacher, Neuadd Welsh).

For some teachers, the discussions with colleagues in which they became engaged had explicitly changed their thinking about their own development as teachers. For example, one said that the project 'created more questions than answers . . . will continue to develop for rest of teaching life' (Neuadd cross-subject).

Most of these same teachers also experienced frustrations and difficulties in the process. Although for many teachers the project experience remained largely positive, for only a few was it without frustration and difficulty. It is in identifying and understanding these frustrations that we can begin to understand how they can be resolved or reduced. Some teachers clearly identified a lack of focus and a lack of shared agenda as preventing work on common ground. Lack of time was cited by many teachers as a reason for problems.

> 'It was more work to prepare . . . we had a lack of time to do it' (teacher, Bont RE)

> 'It was a disappointment. Time was needed to prepare and discuss, but time was not made available' (teacher, Cwrt cross-subject).

Time was needed to discuss and make decisions together in a group, and it was very frustrating when this meant there was insufficient time to give to the project. For those groups, it was as if they had prepared the ground for working together but never really got to do that in practice.

We see from the case studies that the meaning of collaboration depended very strongly on the extent of established relationships among staff. Without such relationships, the experience of individual teachers as part of a collaborating group was sometimes one of getting to know colleagues as professionals, and learning that they were working with related problems and tensions. Where colleagues had already worked together, the project became an opportunity for a fresh look at old problems – or sometimes for the rehearsal of old problems without an obvious way forward. Where collaboration involved meaningful interaction with evidence generated through the process of action research, new turns were developed.

Interaction with evidence

In many schools in England and Wales, inclusion is not a sustained theme; it is in focus at particular moments such as in policy-making, and in relation to critical incidents, and is otherwise disregarded. Rarely is inclusion developed through a systematic and creative process. One useful way of thinking about the outcome of collaboratively owned empirical action research is in terms of *extending the range of timescales* over which teachers seriously considered inclusion: on to the year-long cycles of professional development, and into the minute-by-minute level of decision-making in lessons.

Interaction with evidence involved following the effects of actions over weeks and months, getting feedback from pupils through focus groups or questionnaires. Feedback from pupils talking openly about their experience of lessons was invariably fascinating to teachers:

> 'There was a lot of. . . . Well you get lots of contradiction in what the kids were saying. It's really interesting to see. . . . But it's also interesting to see how they perceive the lessons as well. You can tell that they were truthful in what they were saying and what they said, so that was good. So you got their perspectives and so you actually were aware of what they were saying and thinking about the lessons and that's good. That's where it . . . that's where it started from really. Since we got that, what did they say, it's like they weren't really learning. Learning seemed to be a big thing for them. . . . The best part of it was sitting down and talking with other members of staff and deciding what we're going to do' (science teacher at Hightown).

This teacher might have found such data threatening – given that it is about the failure to engage pupils in learning. He did not, in the context of a group in which the focus was on 'deciding what we're going to do'. Similarly for a maths teacher in describing the framing of their changing practice in relation to pupil perceptions:

> 'How did we know we were making a difference? We did several things. We gave a slightly different form of the original question-naire to the pupils, asking them if they could say in their own mind what had changed in their maths lesson and whether it had helped them. The bottom question was the same as we'd asked them in the orginal questionnaire, about the kind of activity they preferred, to see whether they were more independent, and more confident. And the responses were quite positive, suggesting that we had made a difference to the pupils' feelings about maths. We asked them whether they felt prepared for the exam, and they were positive, very positive. The point that we're at now, is asking them has it been useful, has it impacted on you, are you happy in maths. At the beginning of next year, we'll do the feelings question-naire again, and see if those results have changed' (maths teacher, Main Road).

Interacting with evidence also involved close and detailed observations at particular points, for example, through teachers observing aspects of each other's lessons, discussing evidence of change and interpreting it together.

> 'How the learning of the girls can be totally different to what you had imagined when you teach them. It was really interesting to actually sit there and watch the class. In one of my lessons . . . we were doing group work and the two girls in the project purposefully sat themselves on the outside of the group . . . I was told afterwards that they'd purposefully, *by choice*, sat themselves at the outside of the group to make sure that they did as little work as possible, that they weren't noticed and they just sat there not saying very much. . . .

> 'It's made us choose the focus of our lesson, and it's made you very reflective of your practice as a teacher because you think, well if these girls were not our project or we'd not targeted these girls what about the other twenty-five kids that we'd not targeted? How

does my behaviour and my teaching in the lesson affect their learning?

'Despite the fact that it's thirty kids we've found that the inclusion girls responded well to praise but responded when it was given directly to them on one-to-one basis. It's made me realise that I need to, even in a class of thirty, each lesson I need to find something to praise each child about, to amaze themselves, to make them feel good about themselves in the lesson' (history teacher, Main Road).

Observations generated data that did not necessarily support positive conclusions about the changes in practice, but they grounded teachers' perspectives more strongly:

'How do I know it's made a difference? Well towards the end of last year I actually went into some lessons and did some observations. That was one of the things I told the staff, that we actually looked at each other and while some lessons still fell apart, they were falling apart later on in the hour, rather than at the start. So, you know, it seemed to be a better atmosphere. The students did seem to have some direction and purpose for at least twenty minutes' (science teacher, Hightown).

In Neuadd, to take another example, teachers felt that they had learnt how to know what pupils had understood and not understood, and how to adjust their teaching accordingly. However, when teachers did not feel that they had generated useful data it added to their frustrations, as one teacher at Bont commented: 'Failed to fulfil everything for numerous reasons (e.g. pupil questionnaires were completely unsuitable).'

For many teachers, the action research process represented a sustained attempt to adjust their practice according to evidence of the impact on learners. As evidence from the case study schools has suggested, this endeavour often appears to have changed their attitude to the pupils whom they knew least about, often the relatively disengaged ones on the margins of the class. The changes that were most noticeable among teachers were in their relationships with and attitudes to pupils and classes, and changes in the way they spoke and talked together about the purpose of their work. This will be discussed further in the next chapter.

This section has focused on factors broadly internal to the teacher group. However, no group is an island, and there were considerable differences in the ways in which groups influenced and were influenced by the wider institution of the school. This is the focus of the next section.

Connecting the space to the institution

The advantages of engaging in action research as a relatively small and cohesive group of teachers in a large school are clear. Communication is more straightforward; responsibilities can be allocated relatively easily, and agreement as to a shared purpose is easier to reach. However, there are disadvantages; most significantly, the possibility that the work of the group is isolated from the wider institution, and that when that work ends, the impact quickly fades away. The evidence of the school projects is that structuring and maintaining the space for teacher engagement was insufficient to guarantee impact. In several projects (e.g. Parc, Pentre and Main) the space was well structured but poorly connected to the rest of the institution, and therefore had less impact on the wider institution than was merited. This raises questions about what facilitators could do to increase this connection, which will be explored in the next chapter; and about how the school leadership viewed and impacted on these groups, from their initial formation to the end of the project and beyond.

The initial characteristics of the teacher group were in all cases partly the consequence of decisions by senior management. It was clear that the method of group selection made a difference to the engagement of the teachers. Competition between departments stimulated enthusiasm in Main Road, with other departments coming forward to take part in the next project. Asking for volunteers ensured that participants were interested in Neuadd, while conscription contributed to a level of resentment about the project in Bont. There is a question of group size to consider here as well. The second project at Main Road involved only two teachers, while the largest project involved eight teachers; the average group size was four. In larger groups, participants tended to have more diverse ways of framing the project in the light of their personal history, skills, experience and career trajectory. This made the project more complex but also offered more challenges to existing thinking. Similarly, group members from different subject areas made it more difficult to identify a common focus (Neuadd cross-subject, Cwrt cross-subject) but had the potential to lead to new networking opportunities. Smaller groups were able to meet relatively easily during shared protected periods, as in Main Road, whereas large groups such

as Neuadd had problems finding meeting time, which made organisation more difficult. Regular meetings required the support of senior
management to prioritise and enable them, and this often coincided
with a school culture that valued reflection and the need for 'space' to
work in. Where this did not happen, the project was much more difficult
to sustain in the context of competing agendas, as in Cwrt, Bont and
Neuadd.

Leadership was an important issue: leaders who emerged through
the opportunities presented by the process were often most effective,
having an appropriate style in the context of this way of working. It was
not necessary that senior management lead the group, but where their
'backstage' support was not present, the effectiveness of the group was
reduced. Interest in the project that extended only for the sake of
'inspection documents' (Pentre pastoral) was regarded rather cynically
by participants.

The facilitative support of managers in the school proved to be a crucial
factor in protecting staff time for free periods, listening to and celebrating
ongoing developments, and promoting the project by linking it flexibly
into systems such as staff appraisal (e.g. in Hightown). Teachers'
engagement and project outcomes were celebrated, with outcomes
communicated to and understood by other teachers and senior staff
(Main, Hightown). The ways in which this happened were many and
various. In the first project in Hightown this involved a series of
connections through different brokers, including a senior teacher in the
department who recognised the value of the project for herself; the
continued interest and follow-up of the headteacher who originally
directed the Science Department towards the project, and the performance of the eventual project leader when invited to introduce lessons
from the project to a whole school staff Inset day (to popular acclaim).

In schools with a more rigid hierarchy, the support received tended
to be either too directive or too diffuse, and either way less effective.
Thus teachers' work on some projects was undervalued (Cwrt, Bont),
and the wider dimensions of change proved relatively problematic. The
challenge here is that some shifts are required in the norms, divisions
of labour and communities of such a school, if teachers' projects are to
be appreciated and the understandings and practices generated in them
are to be able to emerge and taken seriously at the school level.
Changing social norms is much easier within departmental and similarly
sized groups of teachers.

We have seen how the mutual influence between the action research
group and the institution of the school depended on some relatively

straightforward factors, around communication, planning, time and understanding of the action research process. We now look to what was learned about sustaining the impact of a project more widely.

Processes for sustainability at the school level

What is necessary to institutionalise the best of a project, creating a narrative sense of agency for teachers, of the ability to make a difference and to be personally engaged within a school in working more inclusively as a teacher? Looking across projects, there were some teachers and headteachers who reported an impact on other staff, and therefore a potential impact on other pupils (Main Road history, Hightown science and pastoral, Parc science). Others planned to continue with action research, either as a strategy to offer to groups of teachers who had a burning issue to address (Neuadd Welsh and cross-subject, Pentre pastoral), or as a way of unlocking staff potential (Hightown science and pastoral, Main Road history and maths). Others regretted the relative isolation of the group involved (Cwrt cross-subject) and had considered how to approach such a process differently in the future.

We noted some significant and apparently simple links that were made in some schools, between the process of engaging in action research and other developments which already had significance to individuals or groups. School leadership teams who offered sustained practical support did so partly by exploiting productive links between different agendas: the action research focus, attainment pressures, the engagement of staff involved and other CPD processes. Such links are typically absent from discussions of development of inclusion, but we found them to be very important in integrating the possibility of collaborative action research into the professional life of teachers and the school. For example, in several schools, the commitment of key individuals to the process was linked in some way to their own perception that it was contributing to their own professional advancement, and in some cases explicitly linked to their prospects for promotion (Hightown science and pastoral, Main Road history).

Linking agendas in this way helped to ensure that staff engaging in projects felt that their participation was professionally valued, and they were then more willing to take risks, feeling supported in working more critically in relation to their practice. By contrast, many groups of teachers felt systematically undervalued when their work was not even acknowledged by school leaders or other colleagues, or where it was not recognised as an important process of professional development.

One example was that of the eventual leader of the Hightown science project. We want to highlight the way a member of staff can influence the practice of other teachers, through a subtle development of their individual ownership of the process, in the context of thoughtful collaboration. Within the project, there was a growing sense of recognition by John and his colleagues of the way in which he had started to influence others, how they had recognised and related to his practice of values and ideas, and how they had felt able to experiment and change their own practice accordingly. The round of applause that John received from the staff meeting was testimony to the practical understanding developed through the project, but it is important to recognise here too the exercise of lateral influence within the hierarchy of the school.

John was encouraged in this developmental role by the discussion of the project within his performance management review. Another possibility for sustaining such effort is the prospect of promotion; but that would be to fit an existing role around John and in this sense is a very conservative approach. We would like to consider broadening the language for expressing what teacher development involves in practice, seeing *disposition to affect change* as very significant in teachers, for example. We see the possibility of John's subtle lateral influence fitting into a narrative of coherent, improvised, emergent teacher development, to set alongside the discourses discussed in Chapter 2 of discontinuous and compartmentalised development, or development according to predetermined standards. A narrative of the type suggested here may in time become recognised on CVs through the appraisal of careful and thoughtful descriptions by teachers of the role they have taken within teacher groups, for example.

Summarising teacher action research to develop inclusion

At this point, we want to summarise the relationships we have been discussing between the processes entailed in collaborative action research in these projects, and the development of a more inclusive context. Figure 4.1 brings together the key ideas that have arisen so far in our analysis of the school projects. The diagram suggests that collaborative action research as conceived and developed in these projects may be understood in terms of three aspects: the pedagogical actions that are developed by teachers, categorised into three groups; the processes that inform and embed this action, which teachers engage in together, and the enabling features of context on which those processes and actions depend. Rather than considering action research as a spiral (see Chapter 2), this framework suggests a more dynamic relationship between what teachers bring to a group (their worries, ideas, suggestions, abilities, experience); the actions they decide to take (working on aspects of their practice in various ways), and the features of the context in which they do these things.

The diagram also highlights three kinds of outcome of this process, both about inclusion. The first is the improved participation and learning of young people, which is the goal of the whole process, and which we will discuss further in the next chapter. The second has been the focus of this chapter, and we will return to it in the final chapter of the book: we consider that the learning and participation of teachers is an equally significant outcome of action research.

The third outcome in the diagram is one that most influences the chance of teacher development in schools changing its character from an institutional perspective. The prospects for such a realignment will be examined in Chapters 6 and 7.

One of the most significant qualities of action research in relation to inclusion suggested in earlier chapters and highlighted in the case studies is that of *emergence*; the sense that the development of inclusion cannot be organised according to a schedule, but that it involves connections and opportunities that are not available or understood in advance. Emergence may be thought of as potentially located in the links between the three aspects of collaborative action research. It is in

Collaborative action research			Inclusion
Pedagogical actions	**Processes**	→	Young people's learning and participation
• Teaching approaches • Learning resources • Institutional organisation	• Joint activity (collaboration) • Group interaction with evidence • Discussing, reflecting, focusing, decision-making • Creativity and borrowing of ideas • Contributions of individuals	→	Teacher learning and participation (re roles, relationships, assumptions)
emergence	**Enabling features of context**	→	**Development of context** Institutional and interagency development which values and embeds these enabling features
	• Group ownership of issue • Diversity of experience • Time • Facilitation of process • Links to other institutional processes		

Figure 4.1 Collaborative action research for inclusion

the emergent interaction between these aspects that the development of inclusion and capacity for inclusion take place.

To highlight the quality of emergence here is to highlight the difference between a plodding and mechanistic approach and one in which conversations may spark ideas and questions, and where these tend to be valued and held – where differences of opinion and experience help in understanding the limits of any one perspective.

Conclusion

In this chapter we have consolidated our understanding of how teacher action research can influence inclusion in schools, and the features of context and process which make that influence more likely. This learning has come about through looking critically at schools where action research was powerful, and at why development was often sluggish. In the next chapter we shift the perspective to the young people who were the targets, subjects and informants of teachers' joint activity and interaction.

Chapter 5

The impact for young people

One of the themes described in the previous chapter was how changing the relationship between pupils and their teacher can affect learning. In this chapter we address this question in several ways, looking at teachers' own evaluations as part of the action research process, and at pupil views on classrooms and inclusion as expressed in focus groups. We also examine the difficulty of identifying and measuring change in these types of attitudes and behaviour and how this led us to develop our own pupil questionnaire aimed at eliciting perceptions of inclusion and participation. Using the results from this and other data, we examine the changes that pupils report have occurred in the teaching practice of their teachers as a result of the teachers' engagement in the project. We conclude that this compound approach is necessary in order to provide some answers to what remains a challenging question.

Teachers' own evaluation of the impact on pupils

As part of the action research process, there was discussion with all groups of teachers about the dangers of assuming the positive effects of changes to teaching and learning processes, and emphasis on the need to reflect on and test those assumptions. Teaching and learning are complex processes, and pupils' attitudes to a lesson are influenced by a range of factors, some of them personal to them as individuals, others relating to the processes and culture of the lesson, and still others relating to the peer group of which they are part. Teachers' own understandings of how their developments changed the dynamics and feelings of the classroom were valued, but we encouraged them to generate appropriate data to confirm or challenge these understandings. Consequently, teachers made evaluations and observations during the course of their research, and used them to guide them further.

Looking across case studies, we see teachers using a range of methods for enquiring into the effects of the changes they were making. For example, 'dartboard' assessments by pupils provided a quick, visual check on perceptions of learning across a class; a pupil comment box provided an opportunity for individual, private, anonymous feedback; and participation by pupils in a 'subject council' provided more sustained and representative reflection. The maths teachers at Main Road explained their strategy for using a simple questionnaire with pupils, and their ongoing response to this as teachers:

> 'How did we know we were making a difference? We did several things. We gave a slightly different form of our original questionnaire to the pupils, asking them if they could say in their own mind what had changed in their maths lesson and whether it had helped them. The bottom question was the same as we'd asked them in the original questionnaire, about the kind of activity they preferred, to see whether they were more independent, and more confident. And the responses were quite positive, suggesting that we had made a difference to the pupils' feelings about maths. We asked them whether they felt prepared for the exam, and they were positive, very positive. The point that we're at now, is asking them has it been useful, has it impacted on you, are you happy in maths. At the beginning of next year, we'll do the feelings questionnaire again, and see if those results have changed' (maths teacher, Main Road).

Teachers in each school typically gave similar responses in terms of what they had done to evaluate the impact of their actions. These are questionnaire responses from six teachers involved in the Hightown science project. The 'Sleuths' mentioned were records of minor misbehaviour accumulated by individual pupils in a school-wide daily reporting system:

> *How did you go about evaluating the success of the actions you took?*
> * Group discussions on grading of the lesson. Peer observations. Shared the findings at a whole school meeting.
> * Looking at the number of de-merit slips the pupils got.
> * Meeting with other teachers in triad.

- Discussion within department – monitoring of Sleuth behaviour forms.
- Monitoring Sleuths.
- Discipline, enjoyment, participation and attitude to learning.

Similarly, their responses on the outcomes of the project reflected a shared understanding of the impact on pupils:

What were the outcomes of your project for the pupils?
- Better behaviour at the start. More focus and order.
- A common expectation for all science lessons. Pupils more engaged.
- Improved behaviour.
- Improved concentration and motivation for a large number of students.
- More settled as they arrived, more learning, better behaviour.
- My students already benefit from a structured and routine start to lessons.

Teachers expanded on this in interviews, noticing how groups had responded positively to changes in their approach as teachers:

'The best lesson I've had with them recently was one on photosynthesis. It was, erm, we were looking at starch. And erm, we were looking at what happens to the products of photosynthesis. What happens to sugar? And we had . . . we were basically looking at starch in potato cells with a microscope. That was probably the best lesson' (teacher, Hightown science).

The data that teachers generated typically gave them reason to see that the effects of their actions were wider than they had hoped. Many teachers reported an impact on their pupils, with target groups participating more (Bont RE, Hightown science, Main Road history and maths), feeling more motivated (Neuadd Welsh, Pentre pastoral, Cwrt cross-subject, Parc science, Hightown pastoral), and attaining more highly (Bont RE, Hightown science, Main Road history). Some teachers also mentioned that their lessons had become less stressful (Cwrt cross-subject).

Pupil views on classrooms and inclusion

In many cases, the pupils involved were asked to participate in a focus group to describe their engagement in the relevant lessons and to look for any relevant changes. In the Main Road maths project, pupils described their maths lessons and some of the changes they had responded to.

> *Interviewer*: Has anything changed in your maths lessons this year?
> *Alan*: The syllabus.
> *Brian*: We do more practical lessons . . . we work in groups, make things.
> *Chris*: When we did probability, we did dice rolling. Then we had symbols on the board, and had to guess which one.
> *Interviewer*: So you've done lots of games like that?
> *Alan*: Every couple of weeks.
> *Interviewer*: Is that the best bit?
> *Brian*: Practicals are a bit more fun, if you can use that word.
> *Interviewer*: Do you like maths?
> *Brian*: No [smiling].
> *Interviewer*: But that's quite fun when you do that sort of thing?
> *Brian*: Yeah. It feels easier.
>   . . .
> *Interviewer*: Can you give you me five more activities that you've done?
> *Brian*: For gradient, we built a ramp along the wall of the class-room.
> *Chris*: Calculating volume, we built a box for Coke.
> *Interviewer*: OK tell me about the ramp first.
> *Brian*: Well we glued paper together, say it went along four, then up two, then we worked out the gradient, and rolled things down it to see how fast it would go.
> *Chris*: For the Coke we had to calculate the shape of a box and then make it so that it would just hold a whole can of Coke.
> *Interviewer*: Didn't it all come out of the gaps?
> *Chris*: No, we sealed it all with Selotape. It worked. We got a prize.
>   . . .
> *Interviewer*: Can you remember those lessons in detail?
> *Chris*: When you use your hands, you remember it; when you use your brain, you forget it. It's about meeting different learning standards.

In this project the teachers were explicitly trying to address pupils' feelings about maths, and they were doing so by responding to pupils' understanding of the sorts of activities that most engaged them. The level of description that these previously disenchanted year 10 boys provide here is significant. At another point in the interview, one boy comments, 'I can do algebra'. The overriding sense was that these pupils quite enjoyed their maths lessons, even if in the interview they were as yet unable to go so far as to generalise this to a feeling of liking maths per se. That the pupils were able to talk enthusiastically and in detail about specific lessons suggests that their teachers were succeeding in creating more engaging contexts for learning. Pupils felt better about maths, *because* they were more engaged and were learning more. As the teachers later commented:

> This sort of data from pupils was very revealing for us, and very much confirmed the value of the process we'd gone through. It's about doing something you enjoy yourself. For example, we took one of Malcolm's activities on graphs to the LEA heads of maths meeting, and they got very excited about it, and it mushroomed into lots of different applications. It's really helped us to be working together, keeping us motivated – working in isolation, things don't move so fast. And that's *exactly* what the pupils were saying to us at the beginning of the year. Collaboration turns out to be important to pupils *and* to teachers. This is a way of working that we would really like to carry on.

There was a more general outcome from pupil focus groups too. In many of the project schools, these groups became a valuable opportunity to try to understand pupils' perspectives on their experience of lessons. Typically, they revealed a consistency and a clarity in terms of pupil views on being included and participating actively in lessons. They wanted opportunities for active involvement; to understand the work; to have and make choices; they wanted teachers who cared about their views, and a mutually respectful and warm relationship with those teachers. Pupils were able to offer detailed and somewhat humbling critiques of the extent to which their experience of teachers reflected these aspirations. The quality of communication between teacher and pupils was a major theme, both where it was appreciated and where it was problematic:

P4:   She shouts too much.
INT. 1: She just shouts too much.
P4:   I asked if I could go to a harp lesson and she refused. Then the harp teacher gave me a row.

> *INT. 1*: So she doesn't really listen to what you say?
> *P4*:   No, she's supposed to let me go. (pupil focus group at Cwrt)

In several schools there were similar stories from pupils about how teachers responded to their feelings, or their lack of understanding. Pupils expressed a very real sense of aggravation with the teacher in the following interchange:

> *Female*: There was a massive chewing gum on the desk where I sit and I put my book down and I said, 'Miss, I can't work here there's chewing gum on the desk.' Well, you can't work with chewing gum on the desk. And she come up and had a look at it and I was like 'there's chewing gum on my desk' so she moved me and she nearly sent me out. She was asking me about the chewing gum on my desk. I was like . . . it's disgusting.
> *Male*: If you ask for help on something and she's just . . .
> *Female*: She'll annoy you.
> *Male*: She just shouts at you lot for just asking the simplest question and doing the simplest little thing that's not even wrong.
> *Female*: Like last week I was absent one of the days and the next lesson I was like, we had this sheet and she actually admitted that she had misplaced one of mine so I started again. Because I was absent I missed part of the work so we had to describe heat loss so I was like 'heat loss of what?' . . .
> *Interviewer*: Hmm.
> *Female*: . . . and she was like, 'you've got to describe heat loss', and was like, 'heat loss of what?', and she wouldn't even like explain to say a flask. She was like, some teachers just like, don't tell you and they'll tell you to try to work it out on your own but if I wasn't here and I don't know what . . . I mean, she told me a flask and I was like, 'yeah, I understand now'. (pupil focus group at Hightown)

The feeling here is the teacher being on the back foot with pupils who are well able to articulate their feelings, and are looking for more positive leadership from the teacher. Another conversation in a pupil focus group reflected a similar level of mutual aggravation between teacher and pupils who are able to compare different teachers' responses and assess the reaction of a reasonable teacher:

> *Interviewer*: Why do you keep getting red notes?
> *Pupil 1*: Because we don't understand the work.

Interviewer: And is that where you get them T?

Pupil 2: Well not just from the Welsh teacher, but if you don't understand some of the stuff you get a red note because you don't understand.

Pupil 1: But if I don't understand in science, my teacher will just let me off and see if I can do it again. (pupil focus group at Neuadd)

On the positive side, there was a lot of appreciation for teachers' humour in class, and the way that this encouraged positive feelings about the subject: 'I like history, because we've got Mr Jones and he's really funny. He tells lots of jokes' (Neuadd).

Simple strategies to foster participation and to help pupils to recognise what they already know were very much appreciated:

Interviewer: Right, what do we mean when we say, 'Do you feel involved in the lesson?'

P1: Like, say if Miss says, 'Do you know any words?' or something to put on the board, and then everybody says one word each or something. (Neuadd)

Many pupils were emphatic about the value that games could have for their learning:

Interviewer: If you could perhaps improve the teaching skills so that you guys could learn better, how would you do that? If you were the teacher for the day, what would you do differently? Is there anything you can think of that you would do in different ways?

Pupil 1: Do more games.

Interviewer: You would do more games?

Pupil 2: Like spelling games . . . long words you don't understand. (focus group at Neuadd)

In one group, the interviewer reflected back a list of what pupils said they responded well to in class:

Interviewer: Shall I recap on some of your thoughts about what would help? – more variety, which might involve more games, maybe using a video sometimes, and a computer sometimes, more group work – helping each other, not working in silence but having some opportunity for background talking, perhaps less homework. And perhaps, if you were the teacher, you would want to make sure that the teacher respects the pupils by being fair, and not just picking on some pupils in terms of either telling them off or perhaps having favourites. (Neuadd)

Again and again, pupils described their sense of engagement with collaborative activity. These girls were talking about history lessons:

> *Pupil 1*: I like doing drama work like, getting into the. . . . Say like when we were doing the Tudors, doing the, like as if we were a Tudor in Tudor times rather than copying out of a textbook.
> *Interviewer*: So what was the activity you were asked to do in role play? What were you asked to do?
> *Pupil 1*: We haven't done any, but last year . . . [interrupted]
> *Pupil 2*: Yeah, it were last year. . . . Thomas Beckett.
> *Pupil 1*: Yeah, we did Thomas Beckett and we did a role play in that. (Main Road history)

Sometimes pupils offered comparisons between teachers who actively sought their engagement and those who did not:

> *Interviewer*: So, perhaps you'd describe to me what the teacher does, that for you, makes the lesson particularly interesting.
> *Pupil 3*: Well it's the way that she teaches it.
> *Interviewer*: Can we try and sort of, you know . . .
> *Pupil 4*: To make it more interesting. So it's not like . . . some lessons, when Miss isn't here, we have like supply teachers. They just give you a page on a book and answer the questions. That isn't really. . . . We don't, it doesn't go in. If it goes in in like a fun way, we'd remember it. (Main Road history)

In focus group interviews, then, pupils frankly shared their views about the aspects of teacher style, social interaction and teaching strategies which contribute to developing an inclusive ethos in their classrooms. Helping the young person to achieve in their subject is part of this ethos, but there are features of the classroom which need to underpin it. Of primary concern to pupils is the quality of *social interaction* between teacher and pupil, seen as crucial to enabling their motivation and participation. Qualities pupils looked for in their teachers included:

- Knowing them and taking time to engage with them at a personal level, using humour and empathy.
- Listening to them, ensuring that everyone knows what they should be doing and that no one is left fearful or uncomfortable because they don't understand.
- Displaying concern, consideration, respect for them and being sensitive to reducing situations that might cause embarrassment and discomfort.

Besides this concern with social interaction, pupils were also very mindful of pedagogical choices made by teachers and the way these impacted on their engagement and learning. Interesting activities, framed in a way that pupils relate to, led pupils to notice their own learning, and in many focus groups they were able to reflect on this in a way that was very confirming of teachers' efforts to develop a pedagogy of engagement. The summary table shows how teacher actions related to the perspectives pupils had on their lessons.

There is a strong relationship here between what pupils appreciated in lessons where they felt included, and the focus of teacher action research projects. For example, pupils valued opportunities for active involvement, which was offered in projects on the use of individual whiteboards, and on pupils setting group targets for lessons. They needed to understand the work, and this was reflected in project work on language aids for Welsh, and on formative marking schemes. They wanted more choice, reflected in project work on learning materials, increasing group work in line with pupil preference, systems for teacher responsiveness to pupil views and in mentoring schemes. Finally, pupils valued mutually respectful and warm relationships with their teachers, and this was the subject of discussion and indirect effort in many projects.

> *Pupil 1*: I'm in top set in geography because I've got a brilliant teacher, Mr Smith, he's always up for a laugh.
> *Pupil 3*: He's funny.
> *Pupil 1*: He gets fun out of the lessons, he's not really strict.
> [Talking]
> *Pupil 5*: He's like 'come back lunchtime if you have a problem'.
> *Pupil 8*: My maths teacher's like that. He makes it easy to understand things (pupil focus group at Neuadd).

In the previous chapter, in viewing teaching as a socio-cultural activity, we were interested in changes in the way that teachers talked with each

Table 5.1 The link between teacher actions and pupils' views of lessons

Pupil views	Examples of teacher projects
Having opportunities for active involvement – many pupils talked about how important it was for them not to be expected to passively absorb what the teacher was saying for long periods of time	Increasing pupil participation by getting responses using individual whiteboards Inviting pupils to set group targets for lessons with a view to achieving rewards Creating 'big maths' activities for pairs and groups, to replace some individual worksheets
Being able to understand the work – many pupils explained how they often sat in lessons without a clue as to what was going on, or what they were expected to do	Developing language aides for Welsh Constructive marking schemes
Having/making choices – many pupils explicitly valued the chance to opt for one activity or another	Offering pupils the choice of learning through different materials
Teacher interest in and responsiveness to pupil views: pupils expressed appreciation of the way some teachers listened to them	Increasing amount and structuring of group work in response to pupil preferences Pupil mentoring scheme
Mutually respectful and warm relationship with teacher – perhaps the most important aspect for pupils, and again many pupils said that this was lacking in many of their classes. They felt that the teacher did not know them well, and that they did not feel any warmth in the relationship. Lessons were not about them as persons	Many projects contributed indirectly to this, because teachers made time to listen to pupils, to engage with them

other; for example, making sense of problems together in different ways, or challenging each other differently. In a similar way, we are able to look to teachers' talk about the difference they were making to pupils. As a result of their work on the project, teachers saw for themselves that they were paying greater consideration to their pupils' learning and participation, and opportunity to 'rethink' their teaching (Neuadd Welsh Neuadd cross-subject, Cwrt cross-subject and SEN, Parc science, Main Road history and maths, Hightown science). They reported a better understanding of class dynamics, placed greater value on understanding how each individual pupil learns, and had come to see inclusion as discovering what works with a particular group. They said they were increasingly looking at lessons from the pupil perspective. Some valued the sustained nature of action research as an extended opportunity to focus on and learn relevant skills (e.g. in teaching and assessment); to engage in teamwork with colleagues, including LSAs; in raising their awareness and understanding of pupil needs; in improving the quality of their relationships with colleagues and pupils, and in their applied knowledge of research methods (Eraut 2005). However, some teachers felt that the project had made little difference, either seeing themselves as already skilled, or confirming their view of inclusion as unattainably idealistic (some teachers involved in Bont RE, Cwrt cross-subject and Hightown science).

Measuring pupils' changing perceptions of inclusion and participation

Pupil perceptions provide a crucial element in knowing what inclusion means and how to recognise that it is developing. We decided not to rely on proxy measures of inclusion such as attainment, because there are so many non-inclusive ways in which attainment figures can be increased. We were primarily interested in the feelings pupils had about themselves within the classroom, and the extent to which they felt they were able to participate and had a sense of being included. Early on in the project, we recognised that there were likely to be difficulties in identifying and measuring these aspects of pupil experience, given the lack of existing, published instruments in this area. Our response was to develop a questionnaire asking pupils to describe classroom practice, called 'What I think about school' (see Appendix). This was then trialled across all projects, aiming to find out what pupils 'thought about their lessons'. The questionnaire had two purposes. One was to provide feedback to teachers directly that they could use to inform further developments. The other was to provide a measure across the different schools in the project of how pupils' attitudes changed as a result of changes their teachers made. This aim was achieved by asking pupils to complete the questionnaire again once the teacher projects were completed.

The questionnaire was designed to probe two related aspects of classroom experience. The extent to which a pupil's experience of the classroom was *inclusive* was assessed through their response to items such as 'The teacher knows everyone in the class. . . . The teacher cares about how I get on. . . . The teacher tells me when I do well'. Meanwhile, *participation* in class was judged in relation to items such as 'My ideas are listened to and used in discussions. . . . I feel involved in classroom activities. . . . I like working in small groups in this class'. Some items contributed to both the inclusion and participation aspects of experience.

We supplemented this by using a published scale called 'Myself as a learner' (Burden 1998). Table 5.2 and Figure 5.1 give the results of these two questionnaires for the pupils involved in the first phase school projects.

The pre- and post-project pupil questionnaires across the first six projects revealed no conclusive trends in the perceptions of the pupils

Table 5.2 Standardised (percentage) measures of pupil perspective for Phase 1 in six schools (high scores are positive)

First six projects	All schools	Bont	Cwrt	Neuadd	Parc	High-town	Main Road
WITAS participation (pre)	61.7	69.4	55.9	66.2	58.1	54.3	65.5
WITAS participation (post)	58.6	67.6	54.0	63.1	52.1	49.9	69.4
WITAS inclusion (pre)	57.7	60.2	52.2	62.5	57.0	49.6	60.9
WITAS inclusion (post)	56.7	61.1	54.4	60.6	54.0	46.7	63.6
Myself as a learner (pre)	58.9	62.0	55.9	57.2	59.9	49.9	61.9
Myself as a learner (post)	58.5	64.2	55.7	58.2	57.4	49.5	62.5

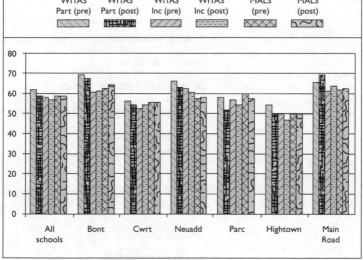

Figure 5.1 Measures of pupil perspective for Phase 1 in six schools (high scores are positive)

whose teachers were involved in projects. The indication is that pupils in the different schools held largely similar perceptions about their opportunities for participation and their sense of inclusion. The changes before and after the intervention on these key measures were small, suggesting on the one hand that the scales provided reliable measures and, on the other, that pupils typically indicated very little shift in their perceptions of participation and inclusion in their lessons. However, the average scores here describe a consistently positive shift in one school, Main Road. This suggests that where teachers were strongly engaged with a project that focused directly on classroom processes, there was a positive effect on the average pupil perception of lessons, in relation to participation and inclusion, and in terms of 'myself as a learner'.

Another way of using this questionnaire data was as a source of feedback to teachers on the way different pupils perceived the classroom. For example, the chart shown in Figure 5.2 was returned to the Main Road history teachers to show them how the responses from the girls they had targeted as relatively disengaged differed from those of the rest of the pupils in the class. The substantial difference in these responses confirmed and elaborated the teachers' understanding of

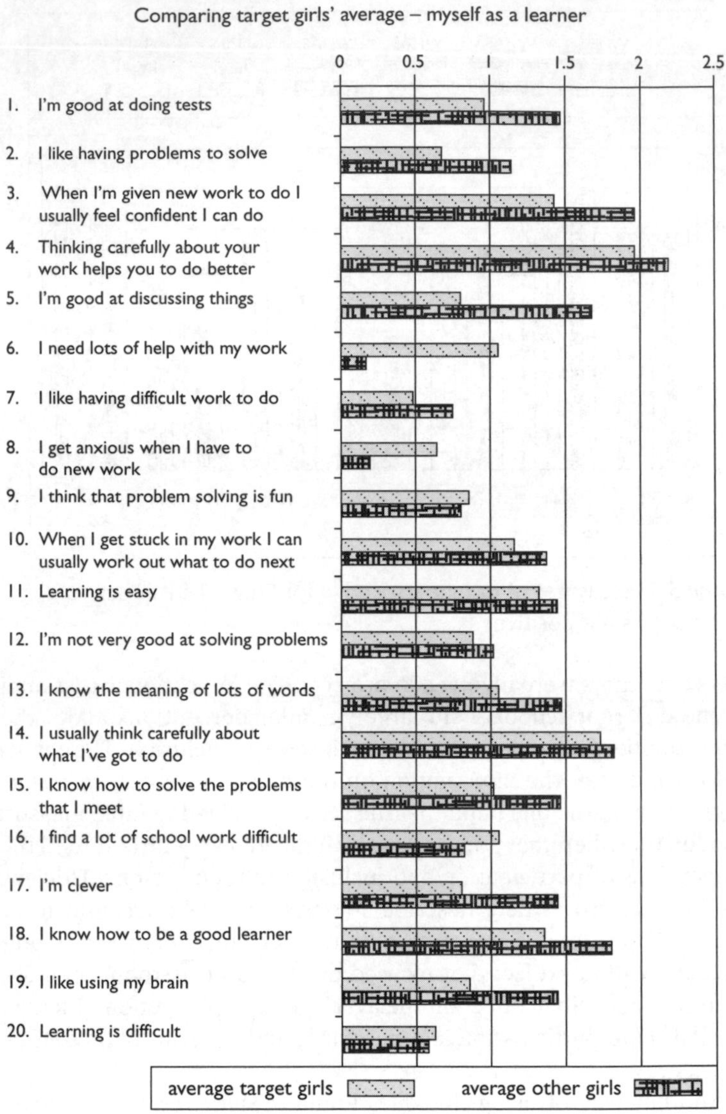

Comparing target girls' average – myself as a learner

Figure 5.2 A comparison of target girls' and all girls' scores on 'myself as a learner'

the group they were concerned with, and helped them to refine their thinking about the issues they were dealing with in terms of confidence in learning.

Charts such as this were very much appreciated by teachers, who were able to engage straightforwardly with such graphic representations, based on their own categorisations of pupils within their projects.

Conclusion

Assessments of the value of teachers' engagement in CPD vary in the weight that is given to demonstrable changes in classroom practice, or to changes in pupils' behaviour or attitudes to themselves as learners, their teachers or their learning (Muijs and Lindsay 2008). In this chapter we have described evidence from a range of perspectives, including that of pupils, to suggest that teachers' engagement with these action research projects usually led to some impact on pupils' learning, and sometimes to dramatic changes. We are not complacent about the evidence we have been able to present; these are difficult claims to make with a high degree of confidence, despite the efforts we have made, owing to the difficulty of assembling data across projects in different contexts. Further development work on techniques of assessing impact on pupils is needed. However, data on changes for pupils also have the purpose of stimulating deeper reflection from teachers, and it is clear that the data presented here and others like them have had a significant impact on teachers' thinking and discussions.

Chapter 6

What makes effective facilitation?

In this chapter we shift the focus on to the facilitators of the action research projects: the educational psychologists (EPs) attached to the schools. We examine the difficulties and pressures that EPs face when trying to prioritise a less familiar way of working and compare the different ways in which EPs have responded to the challenges of facilitation. In doing so we identify techniques that have been effective in these situations to support teacher engagement with action research.

As described in Chapter 2, the role of facilitator was conceived from the planning stage of the research to be central in shaping the extent and quality of teachers' engagement. We believed facilitation would make it possible to create and sustain momentum in a project in busy day-to-day school contexts; it could also deepen the level at which teachers responded to what they were finding. We imagined that facilitation would constitute a substantial part of the answer to our second research question about the features of practice, organisation and external support which can enhance the factors leading to teacher engagement.

As this chapter will show, facilitation can make all the difference to this kind of project, and the demands on facilitators are specific and linked to the critical features of this approach. Many teachers have the capacity to grow in confidence and understanding in the way they relate to and work with different pupils, but as we have seen earlier, this is a process which needs space. Out of the diverse wealth of experience and interest that teachers bring to school, new opportunities for engaging with pupils can emerge – but that does not happen without time, and without the sense that this is a worthwhile priority. Facilitators can go a long way to creating such conditions.

In the preceding TLRP project (Ainscow *et al.* 2006) the facilitation of action research was carried out by research staff in a way that developed as the projects proceeded. In building on this experience in the current project, we wanted to discover whether there were resources already available in the system that could take on this role effectively. In view of continuing debate over the potentially systemic role of EPs in relation to inclusion in England (Farrell 2004), Wales (Welsh Assembly Government 2004) and in many other countries (Englebrecht 2004), we decided to invite EPs to act as facilitators. We saw EPs as already having some knowledge of and professional credibility in the schools to which they were attached, and hoped that the opportunity to extend their work in a more systemic direction in those schools would be a welcome development for both them as individuals and for the teachers and managers with whom they were working. We considered it likely that EPs' understanding of the relationship between teacher and learner, of learner motivation, self-esteem and so on could all be relevant to their role in this process.

In the case studies, it was clear that the facilitation that EPs offered was highly valued by teachers in some schools, but was the subject of considerable critical comment in others. This was quite a surprise to us; our assumption at the beginning was that EPs would typically have considerable experience of practical research to bring to this process, as well as social and relational skills to solve problems as they became apparent. As we will see, facilitation is a complex task, requiring both knowledge and understanding, a clear sense of priorities and the development of a supportive but constructively critical relationship with the teachers involved. At the same time, there are substantial differences in the way that successful facilitation was carried out, which suggests that there is no standard approach that will fit every individual and every context. The aim of this chapter is to build on the findings of the project to identify some principles of facilitative practice in the context of the development of inclusion. To begin with, we will consider some of the challenges that face facilitators in taking on such a different way of working, in the context of sometimes conflicting priorities in both the school and EP service.

The context of educational psychology

A brief historical perspective is relevant here in indicating some of the continuing influences on EPs in the UK. The origins of educational psychology in the UK lie in the development of psychometric testing in the early years of the twentieth century. The first public report on educational psychology, the 'Summerfield Report' (HMSO 1968), traced the emergence of educational psychologists' practice from psychometric test development in the early years of the twentieth century, through the appointment of the first educational psychologists in 1913, to the proliferation of educational psychology services immediately before and after the Second World War. Special education has a strong historical association with medical identification and treatment (Corbett and Norwich 1999), and these new services predominantly followed a medical model of disability and worked closely with doctors. During the 1970s educational psychologists took over the management of this process and continued the deficit focus of assessment, but transferred it to psychological processes presumed to underlie learning (Corbett and Norwich 1999). The psychologist's role was to assess a child's capabilities and very often act as a gatekeeper to special educational provision.

There have been significant changes in society and education over the past thirty years that have influenced the role of the educational psychologist. First, there has been a movement away from a 'medical model' of disability; this began with the Warnock Report (DES 1978) which introduced the concept of integration and has gathered momentum with inclusion now the benchmark for good practice. Second, the recognition that educational psychologists can often make better use of their 'psychology' by developing the skills of others, such as teachers and parents, has resulted in the increasing influence of what has come to be called 'consultation' as a comprehensive model for educational psychology service delivery (Watkins 2000). Consultation 'may be described as a systemic, interactionist and constructionist psychology' (p. 5) which can accommodate work at all levels. Nevertheless, for many educational psychologists the focus of their activity in schools remains individual casework with children (Farrell *et al.* 2005). In England and Wales this is not least because the SEN Code of Practice (DFES 2002; NAfW 2002) places a mandatory duty on educational psychologists to provide evidence for statutory assessments of individual children's special educational needs. Many LEAs are moving away from statutory assessment as the main funding mechanism for SEN; however, in general it continues to be a significant element. A recent study commissioned by the National Assembly for Wales found that over 80 per cent of educational psychologists spend at least a quarter of their time on work related to the SEN Code of Practice; of these, 50 per cent spend more than half their time on this type of work (NAfW 2004a). The achievement of benchmarks for completion of statutory work is an important driver for LEAs which may detract from prioritising the use of educational psychologists for systemic or preventive work.

Some authors have contested that psychologists still tend to work with notions of individual pupil deficit when analysing student failure (Thomas and Glenny 2002). Evidence from interviews suggests that some of the educational psychologists participating in this project experienced tensions that can be traced to their historical role as caseworkers with individual children.

There has been an impetus from within the profession, both in the UK and internationally, towards more systemic working. For example, a recent influential government-commissioned report on the future working of educational psychologists has again acknowledged the potential of engagement at a systemic level for effective school inter-vention (Farrell *et al.* 2006). However, the reality is that traditional child-centred practices have not yet been superseded (Farrell *et al.* 2005; Norwich 2005). Indeed, there are respected voices within the profession warning of the danger that increased systemic working may lead to dilution of psychology within the professional role (Norwich 2005).

There are of course educational psychologists who are able to work on a regular basis at the systemic level. For example, one educational psychology service in our study top slices educational psychologists' time to provide time for systemic work. However, for many educational psychologists, regular systemic working remains an aspiration. Some LEAs feel that schools are slow to recognise the potential of educational psychologists working in this way:

> 'Well historically . . . schools have seen EPs as the gatekeeper to resources and I think we've [the LEA] broken away from that in several ways including the survey and consultation model. But I think old habits die hard and schools very often will focus on the individual child and not see the potential that's there really inside the service for EPs to work more systemically' (Access to Learning Manager, Parc LEA).

The educational psychologists participating in this study were asked to report on the type and frequency of systemic working they have engaged in in the course of their professional practice. Three of the six educational psychologists had occasionally worked in a systemic way to provide teacher in-service training and to contribute to discussions on policy. The educational psychologist for Neuadd School is a typical example. She has worked for seven years as a educational psychologist, and covers a large, mostly rural 'patch' of twenty-five schools, including two secondary schools. She has provided teacher inset sessions on issues relating to autism, behaviour management and bullying, and has occasionally worked with schools on policy issues such as the use of a 'no-blame' approach to bullying. However, she had no previous experience of using action research in evaluating her own work, nor of facilitating a group of teacher researchers.

Three of the educational psychologists had a quite different professional profile and could perhaps be judged as less typical because of this. Two of them had some experience of working as professional tutors on educational psychology training courses. In this role, they had gained a wide experience of professional and field research methods, although neither had previously facilitated a school-based action research project. A third educational psychologist had previously been part of a university project that had used some aspects of action research to develop inclusion in one of his schools. However, even for these educational psychologists, systemic working remained an occasional aspect of their daily work which was still mostly focused on individual casework.

The EPs involved in the project appeared broadly typical then in terms of the limited experience they had of systemic work, generally related to delivering training courses; it was no more than an occasional aspect of their educational psychology work. A recent report on educational psychology in Wales surveyed the perceptions of schools about service delivery. Highest ratings of priority for use of educational psychologists' time were given to individual work with children; research-based work was given one of the lowest ratings (NAfW 2004a). This is in keeping with the findings of a UK government survey (DfEE 2000). The opinions of headteachers of schools participating in this study are aligned with the results of these surveys. When asked about the educational psychologist's engagement at the systemic level, headteachers reported only instances of infrequent teacher training work. Asked if they would welcome an increase in more systemic working, three of the seven responded positively, but gave no clear commitment to doing so; the other four were content for the situation to remain unchanged unless more educational psychologist time was allocated to the school:

'I would [welcome an increase in systemic working] but not at the expense of the main duty . . . to work for the children . . . we have children we know who are queuing at the door and some of them with intense problems. There is a tension there' (headteacher, Bont School)

'No, I am happy for the focus to be with individual pupils – time constraints mean her [educational psychologist's] time should be dedicated to individual pupils' (headteacher, Cwrt School).

As a consequence of this situation, the collaboration of educational psychologists in this study was with teachers whose only previous knowledge of them was as caseworkers.

Clearly then, the educational psychologist attempting to work in a role other than that of individual caseworker is likely to experience tensions over the allocation of time. Within most LEAs, schools are given a limited allocation of educational psychologists' time but they are empowered to prioritise its use. Four of the six educational psychologists in this study found that neither their school nor the LEA would release time from usual duties to participate in the project. In those cases, individual casework was the core work required of EPs, relating to the individual assessment model of SEN. In our view, this amounts to a major contradiction for the role of the educational psychologist in developing inclusive practice, if their individual casework precludes work at the systemic level, given that inclusion requires changes in the social systems of learning. The following specific difficulties were noted by educational psychologists in this study:

'changing professional practice from individual casework to systems work. Particularly when the pressure of meeting casework-related deadlines and performance indicators is always present' (EP)

'persuading LEAs and schools that systemic work should be prioritised during the allocation of educational psychologist time' (EP).

It is important too to note the dominant paradigm of teacher development in the project schools, as this also affected expectations of EPs as project facilitators. Meanwhile, in most project schools, the pressures on teachers to deliver rising pupil attainment scores in the context of busy professional lives and limited time for reflection result in a tendency to prioritise teacher development courses within CPD. These courses were typically organised by private companies and consisted of short, sharply focused training events aimed specifically at improving pupil performance on key exam indicators. They typically involved the quick and efficient delivery of teaching ideas and materials to groups of teachers who encountered them with little opportunity for active participation and reflection. The limitations of such CPD in relation to inclusion were discussed in Chapter 2.

An unintended outcome of regular exposure to this type of training, discussed in the literature review in Chapter 2, is the expectation that satisfactory training involves an expert who *directs* the teacher to new methods for improving pupil results. Teachers may have a reluctance to abandon this model of professional development whereby powerful knowledge is given to them by others, rather than being generated from within their own enquiry (Franke *et al*. 1998). Action research cannot of course be led by an expert; it is facilitated by a critical friend. This can create tension, particularly in the early stages of a project when roles are being negotiated. This tension is further exacerbated where teachers are unfamiliar with the methods of action research, as was the case in our sample of teachers. This accords with findings by Sturman (2005) who found action research to be one of the least common CPD activities for teachers.

Although clear descriptions of action research were given to teachers at the start of the process, many teachers continued to find the concept hard to grasp and the lack of expert direction difficult, until they were engaged in the process. It was clear from the case studies and the chapters which followed that considerable uncertainties arose for teachers owing to their unfamiliarity with action research (Bont RE, Cwrt cross-subject and SEN, Parc science, Neuadd Welsh and cross-subject). In evaluating their experience at the end of the project, there were teachers who saw action research as vague and too open-ended in scope (Cwrt cross-subject, Bont RE). This depended partly on the nature of the facilitation they had experienced. These teachers said that they would have welcomed more initial guidance, and more assistance in generating concrete ideas, as opposed to the broad brief they were given: 'Much time was wasted before the project was decided upon' (teacher, Neuadd Welsh). This teacher's judgement about the value of time spent is extremely significant (Davies and Howes 2006) and reflects a position shared by a considerable proportion of teachers involved in these projects.

The challenges faced by facilitators were exacerbated by their own lack of experience and knowledge of the role. Three of the educational psychologists, all of whom lacked previous experience of action research, agreed that they would have liked more support in order to better understand the skills needed to facilitate the teacher group:

> 'We were given new snippets of theory but that's not the same as going through and understanding the process [of action research]. The EPs lacked that. . . . More discussion of ideas and support for the EP is needed' (educational psychologist).

In deepening our understanding of effective facilitation, it is helpful to consider several cases in more detail.

The facilitator at Cwrt

Linda had been a psychologist at Cwrt School for several years, and was held in high regard by the school. However, she did not have any prior knowledge or experience of action research with teachers. The teachers in the Cwrt project felt disappointed with the guidance provided by the EP ('like the blind leading the blind', one said) and felt that time was wasted owing to a lack of clarity about roles and direction. They expected the EP to be an 'expert' who would direct the new practice that they were going to develop.

In addition, both the EP and teachers struggled to make time for the project due to other work pressures. Some teachers expressed disappointment at the school for not making this time available. The EP commented: 'There is a lack of tradition [in the school] for putting aside time for reflection. It is very much an add-on task. . . . The teachers felt very strongly they haven't had enough time to do the project.'

The broad theme of each teacher's interventions was to use a range of methods to get pupils more actively involved in the lesson, and so take more responsibility for their own learning. They analysed subject topics into more achievable units using materials and methods that were more visually attractive, age relevant and which encouraged pupils' opinions and choices. They evaluated the impact of their new methods by monitoring change in existing indicators (e.g. number of discipline cards, exam and test results), as well as consulting with pupils about their opinions. One of the teachers (an RE specialist) who became most enthusiastic and tried many new techniques reported lots of benefits for pupils including enhanced motivation, improved behaviour and increased numbers opting for the subject at GCSE.

The remaining teacher thought that they had lost sight of the research question, strongly expressing the need for more input from an expert at the start. As a result she found action research unsatisfactory owing to insufficient time and guidance. Even so, she reported some benefits: 'Maybe I'm more conscious/aware of the need to motivate pupils. . . . Gained more positive feeling towards pupils. . . . Pupils more motivated and starting to take more interest.'

In many other schools too there was a feeling from some of the teachers that they needed someone with expertise to guide them, but that their facilitator was either unable or unwilling to provide that. In several schools, the lack of an 'expert' was observed to create discomfort for teachers in the early stages of their projects. Teachers' perceptions in Hightown pastoral, Neuadd Welsh and Cwrt cross-subject reflected the difficulty the facilitator faced in maintaining a balance between taking too much ownership and providing insufficient support. This resulted in some cases in hostility towards the facilitator. The contrasting perceptions of a teacher from Cwrt School and the psychologist about her facilitation illustrate this tension:

'She could have suggested new ideas for us to use instead of us having to come up with the ideas' (Cwrt teacher)

'I was reluctant to be regarded as an expert and give too much guidance, preferring to encourage participants to make their own decisions about how to work differently, emphasising the process of action/evaluate/change in the light of experience' (Cwrt psychologist).

Clearly then there are tensions for EPs in taking on the role of facilitator in these projects, particularly around their own knowledge and skills, the expectations of teachers, and the requirements and needs of school leaders. In several schools, these tensions combined to render the EP relatively ineffective in facilitating action research, as described in Chapter 3. However, this was not the case in all projects. Where facilitation was seen to be effective, teachers new to action research saw it as providing a necessary structure through regular and practical support (Parc science, Pentre pastoral). A facilitation model of distant persistence (Hightown science and pastoral) was sufficient to keep some projects moving forward. In some cases, EPs' particular professional skills, knowledge and pupil-oriented perspectives were valued (Parc science, Pentre pastoral, Main Road history and maths).

Also valued was the broad and long view that EPs had in thinking about pupils' lives in a wider context, for example; but EPs had to be careful that they returned often to the implications for practical action of the discussions they generated (Cwrt SEN). Furthermore, being positioned outside the teachers' chain of accountability helped EPs build a space for teachers' critical reflection (Main Road history and maths, Parc science, Pentre pastoral).

This summary of what was valued is an invitation to consider in more detail the process of successful facilitation. In particular, in relation to the conditions identified for effective action research in preceding chapters, we will explore how four EPs were successful in establishing and maintaining the key conditions of teacher ownership, collaboration, interaction with evidence and reflectiveness. In addition, we will reflect on the methods used to distinguish and then maintain the facilitation role, in the face of other expectations on EPs.

The EP at Main Road

By his own account, Matt's approach to facilitation was disarmingly simple: it was a powerful process involving reassurance, encouragement and prompting:

> 'I think that if you go along and terrify the wits out of people by making it sound difficult, then they can always worry about whether they're doing the wrong thing or not. But if you can just do a little bit of prompting and back-patting about whatever, it's like, "you know it's just what you want to do", and it just releases what's in most people actually, which is about the sort of thing that probably made them want to be teachers in the first place. I mean, helping kids with learning and part of that is obviously wanting to know a bit about whether they're doing and why they're not doing it' (interview).

For Matt, the power of the process lies in his belief that most teachers have a desire to help young people to learn, a desire which may be and often is frustrated by the circumstances and constraints under which they work. In passing, it is worth noting that this idea about teachers' core motivation was also brought out clearly by teachers in the Neuadd project:

> 'There is this thing about your magic C grade and about results, and everything getting analysed. And then sometimes doing things

that keep you motivated and trying different learning styles and so on can be seen as being, I don't know, idealistic in some ways. "Come on, we haven't got time for that; let's get on to the real business." But, you know, that should be the real business, that's the thing . . . and to keep focused and to keep enjoying it, and to stay in teaching. You've got to keep wanting to do the idealistic thing which probably was the thing which caught you in the first place, not these As to Cs' (teachers in Neuadd school).

Facilitation of action research for Matt became an opportunity to create a process through which teachers could recover their own inner sense of purpose. An important principle for Matt was that facilitation should make the process appear more straightforward, not more complicated. So, in introducing the focus group interview:

'There are three main elements which are fairly obvious: really one is describing the problem, two is identifying the causes, and three is suggesting some approaches . . . what your ideas are, what you're doing about it. . . . I'm going to try and stop talking really. Let's go back to the beginning, when you didn't know what the issues were. . . . If you can take us back' (EP at Main Road).

Matt's tone here is typically low-key and informal, and invites teachers' participation on equal terms. In working with the teachers in the two Main Road projects, Matt neither said nor did anything which announced his status as an EP. He took steps to avoid any threatening picture of action research – instead making it appear a natural extension of 'what you do anyway'. At the same time, he had a sharp appreciation of the research process, and an insistence on learning about pupil outcomes.

Matt said very little during the first part of the focus group. Then, as the teachers exhausted their description of the characteristics of the problem, he posed a question from the focus group schedule. 'In what way does it matter?' The teachers responded by expressing quite forcibly the emotions that they feel with the girls. They then began to discuss the difficulties in involving parents, and started to characterise the world in which the girls live. Matt made another gentle interjection, effectively taking a pupil perspective on the issue the teachers were getting excited about: 'You see with me I don't know if I aimed much higher than I needed to go.' At this, the teachers hesitated, with a series of errs and umms and I don't knows. They then concurred with Matt as three teachers trying to make sense of a phenomenon which clearly concerned them, not only as professionals, but also as people working with others. This proved to be a significant moment in the project, reflecting a shift towards understanding these young people on their own terms.

Matt was relentlessly but subtly probing. He was also increasingly enthusiastic about what the teacher group was doing. In turn, the teachers were extremely appreciative of his attention and support. An important perspective on facilitation can be gained from the teachers who spoke about the benefits they perceived in it. It is clear from the comments that they made that they were able to build a relationship with Matt through which they came to rely on him to deepen their reflection, to provide specific guidance on research, and to affirm the value of their developing work:

> 'Firstly, outsider eyes are useful. We're too close sometimes, to our work, to see the obvious. It's wood and trees. Matt has an under-standing of our role because of his role, but he's not involved in the day-to-day classroom things, so he can bring an informed opinion which is more objective than ours. So that is a positive. . . . Secondly, he is good because we were able to consult with him about certainly earlier on, about action research issues that we weren't familiar with. We wanted to be able to establish the baseline. We want to be helpful, we had to have some data to enable us to measure how far we had come or not at the end of the project's term. Matt was able to unpick some of the discussions we were having among ourselves and able to give, from his academic training, information which helped us simplify the sorts of issues that we ourselves were planning. . . . We hadn't got the background to be able to say that I'd done this before, this is how we measured it and this is what we were able to do to establish. . . . For example, we were talking about control groups, we were talking about all sorts of things, data protection, identity with the pupils, etc. Matt was able to give us much clearer views about what we could do. . . . Thirdly, what was very important was his affirming of what we were doing. Every time that Matt was in, certainly in the last several visits, he would affirm what we had been doing. Where we had set off hesitantly in the last year, fumbling and not quite sure where were going and having to find our own markers to set down, Matt has been involved in such a way that whenever we had discussions from November onwards he's been affirming the sort of work we've been doing and that has been encouraging' (Main Road history teacher).

While the critical and technical input was certainly relevant, this teacher's main emphasis here is clearly on the importance of the affirmation that the group received from Matt. This emphasis was echoed in the views of other teachers, including one of those involved in the second project at the school.

> 'The way I see it is, you can't get away from the fact that we are institutionalised. We work with people within this institution all the time. We may go on like a one-day course or a two-day residential, but that's as far as it gets as an outside influence. So it was great having the EP working with us. He was genuinely interested in what we were doing; he would ask probing questions; he would write down what we thought; he would look for reasons why we thought that (Main Road maths teacher).

The value that these teachers placed on the affirmation they received from Matt may be understood in a professional context in which teachers who create and develop a focus as a group are doing something relatively unusual, and therefore potentially exposing themselves to critical comment.

Collaboration – deepening the sense of purpose

From the teachers' point of view, Matt's contribution to the development of their project was significant. At the time this was something of a surprise to Matt, and there are indications that it was a surprise to them as well. It was not after all that Matt spent a great deal of time with the group – meeting with them for an hour on about six occasions over a period of two terms. But the quality of his interaction with them, and the sense of purpose he conveyed, created space for teachers' deliberations, and deepened their engagement. Matt typically acknowledged teachers' feelings rather than dismissing them. He avoiding any sense of judgement, or of evaluating their progress according to a particular theme.

Matt's own involvement and commitment grew over the course of the project in a way that surprised him and led him to recognise this way of working as one that he should prioritise more highly:

> 'Another thing that I am really pleased about in terms of my involvement with the project is the way this has led to me putting this way of working higher on my (and the service's) agenda – thanks!'

Summarising what he found so inspiring, Matt explained how teachers were gaining confidence and enthusiasm as they learned to take seriously their own ability to observe, take decisions together on practice, and reflect on what they were learning about pupils:

> They're animated as well which I think is nice, that's the buzzing bit I think. They're really enjoying having looked at what is going on at this level of detail, I think. And again, I take that to be such a good sign because, I suppose, if I have a set of beliefs, one of them is that the way that people feel about their competency, it's just such an important determinant of how well they do. And if you feel good about it, you're going to do a good job again, without having necessarily an overt plan. I think that's how they came over really. They're just very enthusiastic about what they think they've been doing. Very excited by the things that were occurring to them.

Ownership – keeping it with teachers themselves

Perhaps the most vital element of Matt's facilitation was his serious and infectious enthusiasm for the issue that the teachers had decided to address. He recognised initially that they were engaging with a genuine issue, one that really bothered them as a group. He took that seriously, listening and responding to their ideas and posing some reflective questions from a slightly different perspective. In so doing, Matt helped the teachers to take the time and space to think about their work in ways they were not used to. He communicated a sense of significance to their work, became involved in it, and they responded to this very positively. Matt consistently placed a high value on the process of deliberation by teachers about what they wanted to address: 'A big part of this is thinking what you want to do. Doing that in a small group is easier, logistically' (interview).

Interaction with evidence – valuing teachers' understanding of pupils

It is easy to overlook the value of teachers spending time talking about the pupils whom they see as posing them problems, or to view this as a dangerous activity which might only result in further labelling of those pupils. In an interview, Matt explicitly challenged the idea that focusing on students in this way was a problem:

'In the first project, the group gained a really good understanding
of their target group. . . . They were talking about . . . things like
the gel pens girls arranging their gel pens, but seeing that as a need
for security, and status . . . and *then* thinking about what *they* would
need to change in their teaching to take account of that. It was not
about labelling.'

Matt here upheld the value of teachers coming to understand pupils
better as a step towards working more effectively with them in the
classroom.

Affirmation and challenge

In addition to the ways in which Matt supported teachers in these three
crucial areas, there is another theme that is evident in what teachers
valued in his facilitation, and which he himself emphasised. Matt took
great issue with the notion that part of his role was to *challenge* teachers:

> *Matt*:   I don't think I *challenged* them at all. I think it would boil
> down to me encouraging them in the belief that it's perfectly
> possible to do this, that it's easy when you get down to it. That
> all they would need to do is to think about it a bit. To tolerate
> me coming in every couple of months and to talk about it out
> loud.
> *Interviewer*:   But they obviously do value your questions.
> *Matt*:   There was more of that at the beginning, about what their
> constructs were about disengagement, disaffection – why they
> were thinking what they were thinking (interview).

Later, the issue of challenge came up again:

> I want to come back to this question of challenge. Because it seems
> to me, you can either make this thing more difficult than it is, or
> not. I think people have a little bit of fear of research, and there is
> a danger that that can inhibit people from doing something that
> they are more than capable of. I'm being picky about challenge, but
> if people really feel challenged, in these sorts of circumstances, then
> it is very easy for them to move to the side (interview).

Matt captures an important idea here that fits with our experience from
many such projects with teachers, that the feeling that they are being

asked to do something else difficult is likely to put them off. Action research can easily be made to sound daunting: one of Matt's achievements as a facilitator was to find a way to make it sound 'perfectly possible'. Even so, having built a relationship in which teachers trusted him on this, Matt was able to raise questions with teachers:

> 'In the February meeting, there was a feeling that, we're starting revision now, we have to almost get into a different mode, drilling really. I was saying, sure, I can see that's part of it, but presumably some of the things you've been doing in your new ways of working would be useful, perhaps more useful for some of the students, as ways of revising . . . I never quite understood why it was so different.'

This issue was apparently taken up by the teachers; some pupils later volunteered an example of a memorable revision lesson they had recently had:

> *Year 10 pupil*: Revising fractions. We had a line across the table, and we had to put boxes above and below the line, with the biggest fraction at one end, and the smallest at the other. Then we had to subtract them.
> *Andy*: And did that help in the exam?
> *Year 10 pupil*: Yeah I was picturing the boxes on the table.

Facilitating an emergent process

Collaboratively owned action research can be only partly a rational, planned and systematic activity. It is an emergent process in which possibilities are created and socially constructed over time (Main Road history, Hightown science, Neuadd cross-subject). Clear structures and expectations are helpful, but surprises occur, and the facilitator needs to tap into modes of change as they emerge, by remaining flexible and alert to opportunities (Hightown science; Neuadd cross-subject is an example of when this did not happen). Groups require different elements of facilitation at various times, including consolidating the group itself, asking critical questions, maintaining momentum and sustaining through difficulties. Facilitators need to be responsive without assuming ownership. Their tangential relationship to management appeared helpful here.

Matt's own enthusiasm was maintained by the response of the teachers as they became increasingly engaged in the project they were doing – and this happened in both of the Main Road projects. He commented later:

> 'There was a comment about the whole thing that I really liked. I asked them a question, what are you learning by doing this? The answer was something like, well it makes us think about what we are doing, so it must make us better teachers. The project has focused on the issues of what makes kids learn. . . . What I would hope is, *not* that this would lead to another action research project, but to someone thinking about a problem in a different way – thinking, what is this about, and what can we do – and I'd be surprised if that doesn't happen in the medium term, and indeed in the longer term. It's a problem-solving model, and it could really affect the culture of a department.

A wider consequence of the success of this facilitation was that Matt could see the possibilities of others of his service getting involved:

> 'Then in my own services' point of view, I would hope that many more people would be engaged in mini pieces of research, action research, than they have been. Certainly when we talked about this at the last team meeting, everyone was broadly in favour of the idea that they would each be involved in a small-scale piece of research or action research each year' (interview).

The value of an external position

From a position external to the school, the facilitator's perspective on the institutional culture was often usefully critical. For example, Matt highlighted how the way staff and visitors were cared for in school was very influential in encouraging participation and engagement, instead of blame:

> And I think you've got to have the right school. That's become clear to me because of the school I've taken over, where there is a lot more blaming, and writing off. . . . Where if one were to start a project such as we've done, it would be much harder work because of the school culture. Everything's harder work there, including getting a cup of tea. It's about not even observing the minimum

standards of politeness and care of visitors. They don't look after themselves, they don't look after other adults, they certainly don't look after the students. It's in a very similar catchment, and with very similar standards in terms of GCSEs. . . . That seems trivial, but it's a reflection of the ethos. . . . So it's also about being a mentally healthy place to work, and to learn. You are more motivated as a teacher, if you can see that you are doing something worthwhile' (EP).

This raises the question as to how far these projects were able to contribute to such a culture of care in themselves. There is a partial answer to that in the experience of the Hightown science project, to which we now turn.

The EP at Hightown

Successful facilitation does not appear to depend on a consistently encouraging style and sense of personal support. In the Hightown science project, Graham worked in a less personally engaged way than Matt, typically sending quite formal letters summarising progress in the project and outlining possible strategies that the teachers might use. He engaged in detailed analysis on their behalf, both of data from pupils and also in terms of understanding their own ideas. His practice was to provide clear, written summaries to the project leaders as to how things were going, often using mind maps as visual summaries of discussions or decisions to be made. The following extract from a letter to the Head of the Science Department is typical of communication at an early stage.

'We discussed the ownership of the project. It is for you to decide what you want to do and you are accountable to yourselves. My role is to support you e.g. as a critical friend, helping with data collection, classroom observations, getting pupil views etc. My aim is to work flexibly and probably less formally – but of course I can attend meetings of the staff involved if this is helpful. I have given a list of dates to R and yourself so that you know when I am in school – this saves you having to try and book a visit. It also means that I can wander down to the science department and see how things are going' (letter from Graham).

In conversation with Graham early on, the Head of Science talked about how he felt that there were behavioral issues within the department to be addressed. He also talked about the range of difficulties: from children who are excluded to those who make him feel annoyed by their 'rudeness' and who 'challenge his authority'.

> 'I think we've got two or three things: first is we're a compulsory subject – there's no students opting into us. So if you look at a history lesson in year 10/11 the students have made a conscious decision . . . or a geography lesson – they've chosen to do geography whereas we get every student in the school. Every student in year 10 and 11 will come to us whether they want to or not.'

In the subsequent focus group with science staff, Graham assisted reflection by skilfully summarising where the conversation had gone and encapsulating the essence of their discussions in order that they might think about their practice as teachers and come to an agreed focus for their project: 'It sounds like you're saying that part of the problem is to do with motivation and some of the lessons that you might be giving might be demotivating pupils instead of motivating them.'

In the weeks and months that followed, the project failed to get off the ground in spite of Graham's persistent support through emails, visits and readings. It is hard to see what alternative approaches were open to the facilitator at this point. This time was very frustrating for him, although there were spin-offs in his role as EP. For example, his relationship with the SENCo had become more established, and he had much easier access and relationships in the school.

Four months later, this model of persistent but distant pressure from Graham resulted in the leadership of the project being delegated by the Head of Science to John, the Head of Biology. The headteacher's intentions for the project were no doubt also a factor which meant it couldn't simply be dropped; she leant her status to the project. In all of this, Graham's profile in the school was growing, and he was also learning: he now knew enough about communication in the school to make sure that his feedback got through to the right person:

> 'John did not have a copy of the feedback letter – so we photocopied it again (I had my copy with me). He is going to pass it on to the rest of the team. I have set them the task of deciding which bullet point they want to develop into a project (or if they have another idea – that is okay). They will then decide on which pupils will be the target group(s). I am visiting again in January and John knows that I am going to pop in and chat with him about next steps (I am

hoping that this puts enough pressure on to move things forward). I have also suggested that John contacts me if he wants me to go in before that date. In short, Hightown is not ready to start yet – but they are getting closer.

Graham played a crucial role in framing the project with the head-teacher in such a way that, though new to action research, she could see its potential, and could appreciate the importance of group selection and size. Experience in other projects reinforced the idea that these features were difficult to influence later on (Cwrt cross-subject). Meanwhile, Graham continued to work with John in a similar mode, assisting decision-making by providing summaries of conversations and sometimes suggesting research tools, such as a framework for peer observation.

The emphasis of facilitation in the Hightown science project was not on close engagement with teachers' developing ideas, but on supporting the process of enquiry and the development of reflective action. In addition, the facilitator informed the leadership team and the local authority of the good progress being made by the group. Later on, the coordinator of research expressed some feelings of uncertainty about the amount of guidance offered by the facilitator:

John: He just comes in and smiles at you and makes you feel all small and not done anything. You should perhaps be doing some more, as he's here again.

Andy: Oh right. That's unfortunate that he comes across like that.

John: No, you just see him in the staffroom and you think 'oh dear'.

Andy: It's not about making you feel guilty.

John: Just probing questions without really giving you any hints . . . we're constantly telling the students what to do, or how to do it, or to get around a problem . . .

Andy: True.

John: . . . So, we're kind of expecting other people to kind of give us that same kind of information, like a worksheet. Let's get through the worksheet. Whereas if we're just being given something that's very vague . . .

Andy: Yes.

The contrast between the teachers' open enquiry process with the dominant delivery mode that they adopted with pupils is striking. The approach had some disadvantages:

John: You know, it took us ages to come up with what we actually
needed to focus on. It took us ages to work out that year 10
would actually be the best year to do and where is our problem
and how do we go about solving it? You know, it took us . . .
you know, the other group was . . .

Andy: Do you think it was a waste of time?

John: I think it, I think it was an unfortunate start.

Andy: Right.

John: You could argue that it was a waste of time if we were four
months down the line and the other group was getting close
to finishing.

Andy: Oh, I see. But that's partly to do with Norman [the leadership
of the project]. Yeah, it's a mixture. I can see.

John: In the end, you know, it wasn't a waste of time. Very much
it wasn't a waste of time and it was good that we did actually
work it out for ourselves. Almost like my sixth formers were
doing just then when you came in.

Andy: Exactly.

John: I didn't tell them what to do. We'd just done a lesson on
enzymes and substrate concentrations and rates of reaction. So
they pieced it together and by the end they'd got it and they
were pleased.

Again, the project leader compares their enquiry with the one with
which his A-level group was engaged. This led to a discussion of the
concept of ownership:

Andy: Yes. But it's not just being pleased, it's also feeling it's yours.

John: Yeah.

Andy: I have various people, talking to Patrick and talking to you,
it feels like, you know, there's a pride. It's like ours.

John: But you know, if we do look at plenaries then, you know,
we've got that focus instantly. We're not going to be waiting for
three months . . .

Andy: That's true. So in other words you've kind of learnt that you
need a focus and OK, boom, let's go for that.

John: I don't know, maybe it is the right way to go about things.
I'm not sure. Well it's done now, it's happened. We've got
results so I guess you can't really argue that it is the wrong way
to do things if you've got some success.

Andy: Well, I think it is an unusual way of working these days.

That's true. Except that [taking in colourful and meaningful display work all around the science room walls] I look around your room here and think nobody told you to do all this.

John: No.

Andy: So there is lots of creativity still among teachers. That's astonishing. This has transformed since we spoke last.

John: Oh right.

There is clearly an open question here for John about the enquiry process, where searching for a focus had been relatively inefficient, but which had clearly led to 'results' that were meaningful in the department. It is unlikely that there is any easy resolution to the dilemma around how much guidance to provide in support of a developing group. Interestingly, in the Hightown pastoral project, Graham offered to support the assistant head at a distance, considering him well capable of facilitating the project, and giving a list of the key things to think about. At this point the assistant head interrupted and said, 'Well actually, if you can do it, I would rather you did.' It appears that the role of facilitator involves considerable judgement, and experience is very valuable in making those judgements as a process unfolds.

At Hightown, Graham fostered collaboration through observing and reflecting on the developing enquiry with the coordinators of the two projects, typically suggesting ideas for action, and for monitoring and assessing the impact on pupils. He took pleasure in the way the teachers developed ownership, and put energy into communicating with school leaders about the emerging value of the projects. This case highlights the value of the combination of differing timescales in framing a project. As facilitator, Graham's timescale was characteristically much longer than that of the teachers, and he brought a sustained, systematic perspective, communicated through emails, letters and directly with both staff in the Science Department and with senior managers in the school. This was critical in the face of initial conditions in which there was no significant group leadership available, where the nominal leader was preoccupied with short-term issues of daily practice and keeping up with organisational demands. The issues being addressed by the group were urgent, but lacking in strategy or coordination. The EP's persistence maintained the sense of purpose behind the potential project, until eventually a leader emerged from the teacher group to bring it about in practice.

The EP at Parc

In Parc science, the EP, Gail, was experienced enough to look at the school level to explain the initial lack of engagement with the project:

> 'Where it fits in the priorities is really important. The comp was having an inspection so we couldn't do anything till after the inspection. Then the head was busy with appointments and interviews and so on. My feeling was that, where was it in their prioirity list, when would they get down to this so that we could make some decisions about who was involved, and set up some meetings. I think in a large busy school, with change going on all the time, new staff, things developing and changing, it's the same kind of practical aspect, where is it on the school's priority list, how can you keep it a priority and bring it to their attention?'

Acceptance and warmth

As with many of the other groups, Parc science began discussions with thinking about the problem, and this was an issue they at first found difficult to move away from. Gail realised the importance of acknowledging their concerns as valid and important before being able to move forward to think about solutions. She listened and empathised with their issues but also identified key points at which the discussion could be broadened and deepened.

She understood the significance of acceptance and warmth in a sustainable teacher group, so she also made a regular commitment to bringing some snacks for the group and taking minutes of their meetings. In this way a structure was developed that was maintained over the months of the project, to everyone's benefit. The teachers in the project recognised this contribution:

> 'We've had lots of input, to be fair. Gail has been fantastic. She's been popping in although we've not always been able to be there for reasons being class revisions and things going on. So Gail, she's been really helpful to us. All credit to her. She's been giving us a lot of guidance and she's been giving us papers to read and some of them were really difficult and were really tough to read, but it's been quite useful once we've got through. You know, we've been out of college a while and we're not used to reading a lot of research stuff, so it's been a bit of a struggle, that. She has been helpful' (teacher).

Carrying a 'backpack of ideas'

Gail also saw her role as acting as a resource for the group and provided in this role not only the knowledge and insights that came from being a school psychologist but also researched and gathered information that could inform the teachers' thinking:

> 'I think that my role is something about carrying the baggage of theory. That's what I'm going to do for them. I'm going to know about change theory, and they can dip into that whenever. But the pressure is on to get moving, and I don't necessarily think they will want to do all of that work for themselves. I feel that my role is to be meta to it, but with a backpack of ideas that they can come to if they want to' (facilitator).

However, the backpack of ideas was not simply a way of informing teachers, it was also a control mechanism:

> My control on the process I think will be, rather than running it, having it within a bed of ideas . . . I'm trying to keep a foot in theory somewhere. I don't want to just let it spin along, because that's my feeling that its very very loose. I think that by thinking about theory of change, and experimental design, or whatever, then we can keep a kind of anchor on it, as a balloon. There's a wish for success really, an idea that there will be a successful or an unsuccessful project. I'm worried that they will do almost anything to have a successful project. And we know from research that sometimes the results you're not expecting, or something that doesn't go as well, is just as valuable. I feel that I'll have to keep coming back to things like that.

In summary, Gail evolved a style that drew on her knowledge of group facilitation and research. She appreciated that although the teachers all came from the same department they had not worked in this way with each other before, and it was necessary to develop the cohesion of the group, their collaboration and the ownership of their project. She did this in small 'back-room' ways such as minute-taking, which did not take control from the group but helped to keep them together and on course. She considered that teacher-researchers need some academic resources to develop their project, and to conduct it in a way that will enable them to interact with data productively. However, she realised that in the timeframes and pressures there are on busy teachers they would need her support to collect and make some of these resources available to them.

The EP at Bont and Pentre

Perhaps the most interesting case in terms of facilitation is between that at Bont (RE) and Pentre (pastoral), because each was facilitated by the same person, Marian. She faced challenges from early on at Bont:

> 'It has been challenging saying, it's meant to be unknown, and we're going to plan this together. They've been searching for something concrete from the word go. What is this project about? Just saying that it's about promoting inclusion isn't good enough. Just reassuring them. But I think from my school they've had to come up with something from a very early stage, so that they feel that they can do something, so that they're aiming clearly for it. They couldn't wait for the posters. They've had to, to be more comfortable.'

There was a very dominant person in the focus group and the others all agreed with the focus on language: 'If we crack this language problem we'll be famous throughout Wales.' Their theory of change was that a lack of access due to language leads to disaffection, and that the provision of dictionaries and other compensatory resources would address that situation. This was reflected in notes made after the first meeting:

> Also galloping away in a different direction, 8 teachers [at first meeting all humanities departments involved before it was reduced at second meeting to just RE], difficult to hold together. Senior members of staff to keep it going. They worry about the open-endedness of the project. Their own answers etc. they are quite closed. Welsh language – a main barrier. The key to disengagement. Strong characters in the group – heads of year etc. the issue of time – they want to make resources. RE department. Welsh language with boys is the issue.
>
> (EP notes)

Creating opportunities for new kinds of talk

Marian hoped that a more reflective tone might develop in this group:

> 'Hopefully that they see that they don't need someone else to come in and sort out their problem. But that if they talk to each other, and have someone who's just there now and again. This anxiety about not knowing, if they felt a bit more assured after this, that they could do more by working together – sounds very idyllic. But the anxiety provoked by this not knowing what to do, made me very aware that they are obviously a very led group. If they have a sense that they can reflect and think a little bit about themselves, and if that can hopefully feed into how they teach and how the children respond. Plus, it will nice to have the opportunity to work in a different way. Because you don't get much opportunity, you don't. But if the school perceive that this has helped their staff, then they will see that you can be used at this level.'

Although Marian made herself available to meet with the group to encourage them to think and discuss the issues and their ideas these opportunities were not taken, and the group followed a self-made (or school generated?) imperative to prepare materials and put their programme into action. Marian felt that she may have responded better to this challenge if she had been more prepared. Partly in response to this problem, the Welsh university researchers constructed a toolkit which was provided to all facilitators, and which contained introductions and readings on inclusion, action research and theory of change. Marian felt supported by these materials when she began a new project in Phase II at Pentre:

> 'With the toolkit I felt more able, and wanted to be more hands on. I met up regularly with them in the first term (set-up phase). They have protected time once a fortnight. Peer mentoring was talked about a lot, and one of the quieter and reserved members of the group came up with it as 'something we could do' (despite problems with management over grading, etc.). It was something they had tinkered with, and were keen on doing more about. They had strong ideas about what and why. I've met with them, I don't know if I've been too directive. Gave them readings, tried to get them to think about focus in classrooms, will this affect pupils and how? Year 7, 8 and 9 who might be approaching exclusion. Sixth-form peer

mentors, feeling. Questionnaires for teachers (a sample department), pupils and sixth form pre- and post, and I've been writing
minutes. The project has been running since September – is it on
the right track? Do we need to change something? if we do we can
do it now. We're meeting now roughly on a monthly basis. They are
meeting with sixth formers, learning from them about necessary
changes in September. I've relaxed now and doing less minutes.'

There was a ripple effect around the project. This was a new school for
the EP, and the project helped the SENCo to see the EP differently, and
to think of possibilities of setting up other groups within the school. The
EP also publicised the project more in the EP service. Other EPs were
envious, partly because project time was allocated for this.

Marian was able to reflect that as the meetings progressed, for some
of the teachers involved, the space available allowed the kind of talk to
change it moved away from blame and labelling (a common feature of
early discussions in many groups) to think about more complex
connections underpinning pupil participation. Other things occurred
which told the EP that the opportunities provided by the group were
valued – for example, the behaviour support teacher started to come to
meetings and was incorporated into the intervention plan. As the project
neared its end one of the teachers acknowledged the value of what they
had achieved, and Marian's role in that, by talking about wanting to
take action research forward in the school:

> 'We'd never come across action research. But now we've learnt how
> to do something ourselves. In our opinion, support from an outside
> agency is important. Our school is willing to spend £3000 on inset.
> . . . The school is willing to throw a couple of thousand pounds at
> a visiting speaker but it would be much more useful spending
> money giving time to this approach.'

In summary, Marian was frustrated when working with her first group
because of their headlong dash into action. She recognised the need, if
action research is to be of value, of helping the teachers use the space
it can create for developing their thinking about pupil participation.
The support of a toolkit gave her the confidence to facilitate these
developments with her second group at Pentre. As heads of year, the
group were used to collaboration, but not to having time to develop
focused and reflective discussions. Marian was able to use her skills as
an EP and the resources of the toolkit to move forward their thinking

in this way and enable the group to collect and analyse data in order to evaluate their project.

Conclusion

The EP as effective facilitator in these projects operated at two levels. With the teacher group, the facilitator was skilled, well connected and without managerial responsibility for their work. This combination of features framed a useful alternative space for educational discussion. In this way, we came to see the EP role as refreshing the concept of the critical friend. The differences between the EPs described here suggests that, as with teachers, each person will bring a distinctive approach to the role, using his or her own particular experience to create a relationship that works for the group concerned. This works well as long as the developing approach remains facilitative of collaboration, ownership and interaction with evidence.

The second level of work involves facilitating links between the project and the school, and beyond. This is a distinct activity, and we have seen that some facilitators who were highly successful with the teacher group reflected that they should have paid more attention to this aspect. Through privileged engagement with the teachers, a facilitator moves into a position in which she or he has understanding and insight which can educate school leaders about overlooked possibilities. Simply giving recognition to the work that a group of teachers is doing can open up the discourse of teacher development in the school.

We identified a stepwise process of facilitation to anchor the group process in the management and practice of the school. In **preparing the ground**, managers and teachers need to learn about action research and inclusion to own and move forward with the project. Ownership in school results in more time and resources for teacher groups. In **shaping the project**, co-construction of a project focus by teachers, using theory of change, is a powerful way to build collaboration and ownership. Helping SMT to locate this focus within the whole school context begins a process of whole school interest. **Keeping it going** addresses the crowded school lives of many teachers. In offering a model of structure and forward planning, the facilitator can also foster contacts within and beyond the school, strengthening a project and its impact. **Closure and sustainability** is about embedding the project as a way to address inclusion, by taking stock of what has changed, and exploring links with other developments and activities.

This process is the subject of a set of materials for the guidance of facilitators (Davies *et al.*, in press). These materials were written with EPs as one of the main products of our research (available via www.educationalinclusion.org).

Part III

What are the implications?

Chapter 7

Improving the context for inclusion

This final chapter draws together the themes of the book around a view of what is involved in creating a context for inclusion. We propose a view of teachers as local professionals: active and collaborative learners without whose engagement inclusion must remain illusory. Policy in Wales and England is assessed in terms of alignment with the contextual requirements we have identified. A particular focus is placed on the role of local authorities and children's services in framing and embedding an understanding of the critical need for teachers' involvement. Finally, we summarise our perspective with a call for the personalising of teacher learning.

The findings of the case studies described in the previous four chapters lend no support to the idea that schools become more inclusive through greater awareness of the concept of inclusion, or because teachers talk more about it. What matters instead is that there are conditions and processes available in and through which issues relating to inclusion can be seriously addressed, and where the implications of pupils' and teachers' different perspectives on school and classroom can be realised, understood and acted upon. The case studies have gone some way towards identifying conditions and processes that serve this purpose, and have explored the particular significance of facilitation to support these. In this chapter, rather than postulating about the implications of this research for national policy and for local authorities, we attempt something more humble by considering the alignment or misalignment between the understandings gained in this research about the development of inclusion in schools, and various current policy initiatives in Wales and England, at different levels in the system.

In the course of this research project, we have understood more about the process by which schools become more inclusive. We note, for instance, that many of the metaphors used for development fit poorly with the concept of inclusion with which we are working. Inclusion is not a product to be *promoted*, like a new film or a cheese. Inclusion necessarily involves teachers in going beyond standard practices in teaching and learning, to engage learners for whom standard practices seem not to work. This requires a focus on what it is about standard ways of doing things that don't work so well for those pupils, and finding ways to change those practices. This project has been about identifying a methodology through which teachers can explore for themselves alternatives to the practices that fail to serve all pupils. It is also about identifying possible resources in the system which can make this doable. Chapters 3 and 5 demonstrated how pursuing such a process helped to re-engage some pupils with education in a range of subjects and contexts.

Part of the challenge here is that standard practices are relatively safe, not necessarily in themselves, but because they come with a weight of association and common assumptions: taken-for-granted connections, common-sense rationales, and tried-and-tested resources. In addition, variation from standard practice is subject to critical scrutiny within current accountability regimes, especially in conditions where educational outcomes are relatively low. Changing standard practices means making other connections, constructing different rationales, identifying other resources. Alternative practices require a clear justification, so that going beyond standard practice involves risk-taking. Many of the school staff in our case studies evidently felt this risk all too clearly, and much of Chapters 4 and 6 described how this sense of risk could be mitigated.

We do not contest the view that pupils' experience of education is influenced by the systems, structures, philosophy and values that underpin the thinking and discourse of education. There is much proper emphasis on the value of changing structures in order to achieve developments in schools: arguments based on the limitations of relying on teachers' best intentions, for example. This is not to say that teachers are any less reliable or courageous than anyone else, but simply to note that optimism about individuals making a difference is likely to be naive where those individuals are embedded in an intricate community web of norms and taken-for-granted goals. Certainly there is a strong case for using changes in structures in order to develop a more inclusive system; through, for example, changes in curriculum, assessment and pedagogy. The profound influence of assessment on the way the curriculum is approached is well documented and understood, for example, and sometimes this understanding influences policy and practice in schools. The concept of Learning Pathways in Wales, which is intended to personalise the learning experiences and assessment of each individual 14- to 19-year-old: pathways are intended to be individually tailored, offering wider choice and flexibility, and giving all learners the support of a learning coach. The revised KS3 curriculum in England, for example, is being developed with the goal of educating learners who enjoy learning, make progress and achieve; confident individuals who are able to live safe, healthy and fulfilling lives, and responsible citizens who make a positive contribution to society. That the curriculum can influence the structure and organisation of schools is evident in the dramatic loss of music, arts and humanities in English primary schools that was associated with the introduction of the literacy and numeracy strategies (Boyle and Bragg 2006).

However, the case being made in this book is that a context for inclusion depends not only on structures, but also on teachers being engaged in thinking about and understanding their pupils, and changing their practice in response. The approach explored here is an iterative or cyclical process through which teachers can learn together about the difference they make, and can make, to the experience of pupils in their classrooms. There is no denying that inclusion depends on structures, but it is crucially influenced by the intimate experiences of everyday lives in school, in which classroom experience features very strongly.

These two levels of structure and everyday experience are intimately linked. Activity by teachers generates discourse in which problems are discussed, and in which pupils are better understood. Pupils, and how to work to include them, are the subject of conversation – and as this conversation becomes part of the school, it influences the way aspects of school organisation are perceived, understood and evaluated. Case studies and teacher interviews showed how unusual most teachers felt it was to have time set aside for focused and reflective conversation, and as we saw in Chapter 4, this was one of the aspects that they most valued. In several of the project schools, it was evident even in a short period of time that this process contributed to changes in school organisation, such as the development of reward systems at Main Road, and the construction of further opportunities for teacher-led development in Hightown and Pentre.

In this book, we have viewed collaborative action research as a structured process through which teachers are supported in attending to and developing the context of learning in their classrooms. We are interested in how to create and contribute to a context for inclusion, and the last four chapters have demonstrated the distinctive value of collaborative action research in providing a way for classroom teachers to address everyday classroom issues together, and in creating a space in which teachers are able to examine and move beyond assumptions and current practice. We have seen how this space should be characterised by the flexibility and informality which allows the creative emergence of ideas and practices.

Flexibility, informality and emergence are necessary qualities of this process, but they also increase the risk that this process is misunderstood and misrepresented. By contrast, well-elaborated and stepwise processes are easier to describe and to train people to implement. To take account of this risk, we employ four tactics in this final chapter to draw attention to vital features of this process. First, a particular view of teachers is described which is congruent with the processes we have described. Second, some current policies are assessed in terms of how they align with what is proposed here. Third, resources are identified which could be used to facilitate more activity, and fourth, these sections are drawn together through a comparison between the proposed approach and the notion of personalised learning.

A view of teachers as 'local professionals'

In Chapter 1, we discussed the way in which teachers are not typically part of multi-agency working. Work on the Every Child Matters agenda, for example, is usually the province of agencies outside the school working with school leaders: it has an impact on the organisation of the school, but not generally on the classroom. By contrast, this research has demonstrated the value of a strategic relationship between teachers and educational professionals outside the school; a relationship which need not be time-consuming but which has the potential to inform and change the understandings of all the parties involved.

The third report from the Centre for Equity in Education (CEE 2008) tackles the significance of local context in identifying some principles for equitable reform, where dialogue between stakeholders is seen as an essential process leading to deeper shared understanding and need for action. They point to a need for alignment between interagency structures and local issues, and for a broadening of accountability beyond individual services. These features have been evident in the work done by teachers and educational psychologists in our case studies, albeit in limited ways.

In the CEE report, the term 'local professional' is used to designate the many people who are professionally involved in the interests of the people and activities in a local area. These are seen as including social workers, police, local authority officers and headteachers, for example. We see our work as contributing to an extension of this term to include teachers, not because we think that teachers should become social workers, but to signify the position that many teachers occupy in the lives of children and young people. One way of viewing the changes that have occurred for teachers in these projects is that they started to see themselves as having access to local knowledge and understanding, often through talking with and thinking about pupils, which they could put to good use in their classrooms.

In viewing teachers as local professionals, we draw attention to three important qualities of teachers that have been elaborated and confirmed in this project: teachers as active learners, situated and collaborative learners, and as networkers-in-context.

Teachers as active learners

There is a view that teachers find it difficult to change; that they change only when conditions force them to do so. On this view, inclusion can only develop in schools to the extent that it is possible to change school structures. Our experience in these projects is that this is a partial view. Certainly changes in structures are important, because change entails risk for teachers, and because there is a momentum behind the status quo. But the projects have highlighted many teachers as active learners, making sense of the challenges they face by drawing on many diverse ideas and experiences. Action research as practised in these projects is not a technical fix, but then inclusion is not waiting for one. Instead, engaging in an action research process has involved teachers in issues that go well beyond a narrow view of young people as pupils. Teachers have grappled with the relationship between language and identity, with their ideas about social class, and the way these issues influence the pedagogic relationship between teacher and pupil. In at least two schools, teachers found themselves reconsidering ideas about peer groups, and about the positioning of pupils within the school community. In several cases, a significant outcome of projects was the way that they fostered a culture of teachers' self-efficacy.

Teachers as situated and collaborative learners

Our work lends emphasis to the notion of teachers whose learning is situated in a particular institutional context. More than that, the immediate social context in which teachers work is crucial to their identity as learners. Our evidence supports the idea that if what is valued and aimed for comes to be shared in that immediate context, it can become embedded and sustained. In several projects, the ideas of individuals became shared as those individuals became more central members of the department or group of teachers. This process has been theorised by Lave and Wenger (1991) in their concept of community of practice, as explained here by researchers studying school and industrial workplaces:

> Lave and Wenger want to stress that a community of practice is not merely a repository for the technical knowledge and skills entailed in the community's activity (e.g. tailoring or midwifery), rather they see it as 'an intrinsic condition for the existence of knowledge, not least because it provides the interpretive support necessary for making sense of its heritage' (p. 98). Put another way, they view the knowledgeable practitioner not only as someone who commands and can apply the necessary knowledge and skills but who, through their membership, has become a full participant in the cultural practices of the community.
>
> (Fuller *et al*. 2005, p. 52)

This situated perspective lends what we view as appropriate weight to the significance of the social in professional learning, suggesting that 'a community of practice is a necessary condition for status and practice of experienced professionals' (Colley 2007, p. 178).

This relationship between participation, knowledge and community engages with the quality of emergence that we found in successful projects: the way in which the priorities and ideas of individuals and of the group consolidated and shaped each other, often leading in unexpected directions. The question of whether the individual or the group comes first in this development is the wrong question, just as with the chicken and the egg. What is much more important is to avoid killing the chicken or breaking the egg – it is the life of the project which matters, situated in the movement of knowledge and knowing between individuals and groups. This life emerges and develops in a necessarily situated process, and the job of anyone interested in furthering such a process is to approach it with a view to understanding and supporting this process, rather than imposing an external framework for learning.

Case studies support the finding in other studies that the wider institutional context greatly influences this social-cognitive process of learning. In a study of teachers' professional community in twenty-four schools, Louis *et al.* (1996) demonstrate that:

> [T]he phenomenon of 'schoolwide professional community' both exists and varies considerably between schools. . . . The data also imply that professional community emerges more readily in some contexts than in others. Many of the factors that appear to support professional community are 'manipulable' in the sense that policy and administrative practice can engender them. Both structural conditions and human and social resources are important. Other factors, such as changing the different cultures associated with school level, are less malleable.
>
> (Louis *et al.* 1996, p. 785)

We looked to educational psychologists to help shape the structural conditions in a favourable way, facilitating collaborative processes and ownership of action research, rather than trying to directly influence the institutional culture. The work of teacher groups and educational psychologists could in some cases be described as 'extended collaboration' (Centre for Equity in Education 2008, p. 25; and Table 7.1), involving the development of a strategy, the identification and validation of local priorities, and generating an interest and need for deeper understanding of context. In our experience, the sharing of values and priorities is usually a consequence of extended collaboration rather than a condition for it, and the relationship between these elements of extended collaboration is what we describe as emergence.

This distinction between restricted and extended collaboration is another way of discussing what was evident in several case studies, that not everything in the name of collaboration actually involves individuals or individual groups in reaching beyond the boundaries of their custom and practice. The concept of networking needs to be approached with a similar sense of caution.

Teachers as networkers-in-context

The successful projects involved teachers working together with a external educationalist, engaging in critical questioning, and establishing a

Table 7.1 'Extended collaboration'

Restricted collaboration	Extended collaboration
Partners focus on their own targets	Partners share priorities and values
Collaboration is restricted to mutual support at the margins	Collaboration supports a shared strategic approach
National targets are used to set local priorities	Local priorities arise from an analysis of the local situation
Analysis is restricted to reviewing local performance on national measures	Analysis is concerned with a deep understanding of the local context

Source: Centre for Equity in Education (2008, p. 25)

more informed and localised educational discourse for more inclusive practice within their department. Networking around this process began with a local exchange of perspectives, characterised by honesty in relation to challenges in the classroom, and understanding based on shared knowledge of pupils, classes and school context. As we saw in Chapter 2 however, networking is often seen as a way of freeing knowledge and understanding to be shared much more widely. We want to suggest that networking is valuable to the extent that it builds on a shared context.

Sometimes the knowledge and understanding generated in a project travelled out beyond the context in which it was originated. Towards the end of the Main Road history project, for example, the Head of Department, Anne, was invited to visit another school to discuss their project with a teacher of design and technology. This invitation came about through a series of connections. Main Road was part of a *Leadership Incentive Grant (LIG)* cluster. LIG grants were made available to schools in disadvantaged areas, clustered as part of the *Excellence in Cities* agenda in England between 2002 and 2006, the aim of which was to foster the development of school leadership for improving attainment and to contribute to greater equity through collaboration. Anne's 'old deputy head' had been seconded to the local authority to lead the LIG cluster, and chaired its meetings: 'so I went along to one of them and told them . . . it was other deputy heads and sort of assistant heads in teaching and learning and things like that, and we just talked to them about [the project].'

Then a deputy head who had been at that meeting returned to her school and mentioned Anne's project to her Head of Design and Technology. This teacher subsequently invited Anne to visit her department:

> 'So I went into [her school] one morning and spent the morning with her there, going through the project and talking to her about the project. She was, she's quite a forceful character, quite a strong woman and she was really bothered in D & T with them [a group of girls] producing really pretty stuff that had no content. Even more so in something like D & T. Also, she was quite concerned with the girls being very girly and she didn't like . . . she said she was getting a lot of the girly girls who didn't want to get involved in D & T because they thought somehow, you know, not feminine enough for them or something.'

Anne's interpretation of the visit was inconclusive as to its value to the teacher concerned:

> 'I don't know if anything came out of that, no. 'Cos she said, erm, she said that she thought other heads of department at [her school] would be interested. I offered, you know, I said well I'd be quite happy to come along and talk to anybody if they want. She didn't get back to me so I don't know whether she did do anything or not. . . . Certainly, at the time, she said it linked in with a lot of her problems producing lack of stuff and not actually having any, well, meaning or measure to it, so. . . .'

This series of connections illustrates the flow of networking, and the desire for effect that new connections often bring with them. Anne wanted the visit to have been meaningful, reflecting the optimistic opportunism that networking suggests. Without the network structures in the local authority, and the associated brokering of two deputy heads, there would have been no opportunity to link with a head of department in another school addressing similar issues, and not even the possibility of further professional development. In terms of meetings. exchanges and conversations, this second stage of networking worked (Frankham 2006).

However, Anne's visit led to no continuing dialogue; after a sharing of similar problems, and a mutual concern, she ended up with only doubts about the value of her visit. These doubts stand in stark contrast with the confidence expressed in the development in her own department. There was, in practice, no mutual accountability in the relationship between the two heads of department, and only a hope that the visit might have born some fruit in terms of teacher development. Despite the energy that Anne put into it, and in sharp contrast to our claims for the value of the projects within school, it is difficult to have any confidence about the effects of this element of networking.

Our conclusion is that networking is an important element of action research, to the extent that the context of knowledge and understanding being shared is not lost. One approach which has proved useful (Ainscow et al. 2006, pp. 140–141) is to invite teachers from other schools to visit, and during the visit for them to be actively involved in the action research process, for example, by observing pupils in lessons and afterwards interviewing them, then feeding back what they find to the host teachers.

To see teachers as local professionals is to give emphasis to their active involvement as collaborative learners, located in a particular community and institution but developing their practice partly through meaningful connections in a network of other educational professionals.

The alignment of policy, structures and practices with this approach to teacher development

In this section, some current policies in Wales and England are examined in terms of how they align with the findings of the research. In this way, we direct the focus of attention on the interaction between these policies and the people who are implicated within them. We use the framework created in this study to understand the relevance and likely impact of particular policies on this approach to the development of inclusion.

Increasingly distinctive educational policies in Wales and England contribute to differences in alignment with this approach in these two countries. In Wales, evidence is increasingly available on 'the processes through which education policies are formed . . . [and] the nature of the policies which are adopted' (Rees 2007, p. 8). Commentators have concluded from both policy formation processes and from the content of policy that 'the distinctiveness of Welsh education policy should be interpreted as a continuation of established, social democratic policy themes; in contrast with the radical changes being effected by New Labour in England' (Rees 2007, p. 8).

There is an increasing sense of Wales as a distinctive educational place (Daugherty and Davies 2008), characterised by self-determination in generating a distinctive discourse around educational purpose. Most visibly, a relatively common history and culture in Wales has made it possible to create a powerful narrative around the idea of the 'Learning Country' (NAfW 2001), and this been followed by *Learning Country: Vision into Action* (Welsh Assembly Government 2006) which reaffirms and updates this vision. There is of course fragmentation of this narrative, but to a lesser degree than would be conceivable in England. In introducing this ground-breaking policy document in 2001, the then Welsh Minister for Education Jane Davidson made sense of the Welsh context by contrasting partnership and collaboration with an implicitly English focus on competition, and by contrasting local support and professional judgement with centrally driven agendas:

> The document sets out how I intend to promote Wales as a learning country – making the most of partnership and collaboration that is evidence based, locally supported and professionally valid. It steers away from a basic reliance on centrally driven, competitively inspired, and community damaging approaches.
>
> (Davidson 2001)

Both documents strongly advocate the benefits of localism in relation to communities which included a strong Welsh commitment to the role of local authorities and comprehensive secondary schools: 'Our communities want excellent local comprehensive schools for all their children. Partnership on that front is at the heart of the way we do things in Wales' (NAfW 2001, p. 1).

Commenting on this element within the *Learning Country* document, Daugherty and Jones (2002) note:

> Under the equally significant chapter heading 'Comprehensive education and lifelong learning in Wales' can be found statements that many would applaud as celebrating what is already distinctive about education in Wales. The commitment to a system of non-selective comprehensive secondary schools is expressed in startlingly direct terms.
>
> (Daugherty and Jones 2002, p. 109)

The approach to diversity in the high school system that is being taken in Wales differs strikingly from that being followed in England. In Wales, diversity is to be addressed within each school, and the emphasis is on the quality of comprehensive education in those schools. In England, the development of specialist schools embodies an intention to address diversity in an offer of school choice. There is heated debate about the merits of such an approach in relation to inclusion (Thrupp 2006).

Educational policy becomes influential when it concerns core processes in schools, so it is important to consider the extent of changes in policy on assessment and curriculum.

Assessment policy

Currently, there are moves in both Wales and England to reduce the extent to which young people are judged on the basis of outcomes in a narrow set of examinations. The Welsh Assembly Government, following the Daugherty Review (NAfW 2004b), took the first step of phasing out standard assessment tests (SATs) for pupils, and moderated teacher assessments are being developed as the main source for evaluating pupil progress. England has followed suit with regard to 14-year-olds. There is an alignment here with the project in two respects. First, where the engagement of young people in education is a valued outcome in itself, it is detrimental to focus unremittingly on narrow academic attainment. In the project, we decided not to look for evidence of impact on GCSE results across the project, based on the difficulties experienced in other projects of demonstrating any causal influence, but also in recognition of the need to find out about learner engagement more directly. Chapter 5 gave some pointers towards these, and some sense of how they might be monitored. Speaking about what is valued is insufficient; there must be implications for assessment practice.

Second, the end of testing at KS2 in Wales removes an important measure which informed an overly simplistic comparison and therefore competition between primary schools, and allows primary schools more freedom to focus on the outcomes of education which they consider to be valuable. Unfortunately, such fundamental questions are unlikely to be addressed when so much leadership and management effort focuses around performance. In the projects studied in this research, and despite the rich engagement with learners that was created, the focus on performance was never far away. Often it had the effect of drawing debate to a close, sterilising the educational discourse that was emerging:

> 'I think that's probably another knock-on thing that I've learnt is last year I made that our focus and that was our departmental thing for the year so this year I have done the same, that we have one thing for the year. . . . My theme for this year was originally assessment for learning which we decided together. Each of us had a different

focus but then we changed it [laughter]. We changed it on Monday because we had quite disappointing GCSE results. [The theme this year] will be GCSE results. As simple as that. GCSE results. Chris is going to look at essay writing. I'm looking at skills and Steve's going to look at doing more games and things to improve knowledge, because our kids do really well at skills' (Head of History, Main Road).

In terms of our teacher development framework, what is threatened here is the ownership of an issue by staff, where a theme decided together (AfL) is abandoned in a day in response to GCSE results. Reducing the pressure on schools to perform in examinations is likely to give more opportunity for groups of teachers like this to focus on fundamental and contextually significant educational issues.

Curriculum change

Another driver of change which currently lies in the hands of policy-makers in Westminster and Cardiff is the curriculum. In general terms, the more inflexible a curriculum, the less regard it pays to the engagement of learners as developed in Chapter 1. Policy changes towards a more flexible and responsive curriculum therefore align with a more inclusive approach, and there are promising signs in the development of a curricular framework which embodies at many levels the aim of inspiring and involving children and young people. For example, in Wales the experiential and play-orientated Foundation Phase is being rolled out for 3- to 7-year-olds (Siraj-Blatchford *et al.* 2007), and in upper secondary and post-compulsory education the *Pathways 14–19* programme (Welsh Assembly Government 2005) has established a policy and practice framework within which a new curriculum and qualification, the 'Welsh Baccalaureate', is being introduced (Hayden and Thompson 2007).

The alignment of the outcomes of the project with these policy changes in assessment and curriculum are clearly welcome. In themselves though, they pose significant questions about the readiness of staff in schools to embrace the opportunities that are created to become more responsive to learners. There is significant evidence that relaxation of central government directives on teaching and learning is insufficient to create meaningful change in classrooms where teachers feel accountable for the detail of their practice. One relevant and heavily researched case here involves the literacy hour in England, and the dilemmas introduced when teachers followed the strategy, almost literally, to the letter, while paying much less attention to the way pupils responded in their written work:

> These dilemmas become more acute when the local account-ability culture stresses compliance with the central direction of the Strategy and meeting its apparent demands over and above problem-solving the specific set of conditions that arise in local settings as implementation occurs.
>
> (Moss 2004, p. 130)

The projects we researched demonstrate that the development of teacher engagement is possible, and powerful in its effects – but also reveal much about the significant processes and supportive structures that are required in schools to facilitate this development. The framework developed in the project may be used to test and improve the readiness of schools to support such processes.

As we saw in Chapter 1, there is also considerable policy effort in the area of services for children, and this is another area of significance in terms of the research findings.

Personalisation, children's services and teacher development

As coordination between services for children has become embedded in changes in local structures in England and Wales, managers and organisers of services relating to children are talking together regularly who earlier had very little contact. In many local authorities this involves services being relocated into shared buildings, where there are typically regular joint meetings and managerial discussions regarding resources and priorities. These are generally perceived to be valuable in terms of the coordination of effort and focus across the authority:

> Where the interviews and contextual evidence suggest that integration is more mature, the study indicates that this is particularly associated with:
> * the quality of working relationships and communication between agencies
> * having a clear and shared vision
> * having fewer concerns about models of funding and associated accountability.
>
> (Lord et al. 2008, p. 5)

Considerable effort is going into the rhetorical work to align ways of seeing things, and to develop more common language. Nevertheless, this multi-agency activity often still feels like a thin crust of pastry on the education pie. Teachers and pupils are not greatly involved or engaged; they experience 'Every Child Matters' as rhetoric, and largely lacking significant implications for everyday practice (Lord *et al*. 2008, p. 5). With regard to the development of extended schools, for example, the only case of significant connection between teachers and the 'extended' approach is in terms of the offer of an adapted curriculum for some groups of pupils (Pearson *et al*. 2007).

The significance of teachers' involvement with other professionals in working most effectively with children and young people who are relatively marginalised or at-risk is signalled in frameworks of teacher standards. In terms of approaches, the professional development standards for new and serving teachers place expectations on teachers to collaborate in the following terms:

> analyse and reflect on their own practice in order to improve learning and teaching. They seek to improve their practice through professional development including engaging with and contributing to the development of new knowledge and ideas. In recent years the field of education has been characterised by innovation and change. Teachers use their experience and professional judgement to assess the benefits of adapting their practice through critical analysis of any innovative pedagogy, strategy or theory. In the context of new professionalism teachers find themselves increasingly both developing their skills as coaches and mentors, and benefiting from the coaching and mentoring that they receive.
>
> (TDA 2007)

These standards are written without an explicit methodology, but there are methodological implications in the notion of standards for individual teachers. What comes across here is the individual teacher focus in standards which are about analysis, change and collaboration. The implicit model of change supports the notion of teachers as active learners, but the roles allocated to teachers as learners are narrow and individualistic, involving 'analysing and reflecting on their own practice' and 'adapting their practice'. Collaboration is understood as limited to the constrained roles of coaching and mentoring, and there is no sense of groups of teachers or departments as having any significance in the development of professional discourse and action.

There are other policies that affect the landscape of inclusion in particular ways. Data from the predominantly Welsh-medium schools (Bont and Cwrt) suggest that teachers' concerns about pupils' Welsh-language skills influenced much of their thinking about inclusion, and led to the identification and construction of problems in similar ways, for example, in terms of the need to redress the deficiencies in pupils whose home language was different to that of the school. In a similar way, we found that although local authority representatives were familiar with a broad conception of inclusion, their accounts of practice and resource distribution were all heavily influenced by the discourse of special educational needs. Where there are dominant discourses such as these at work, engaging with pupil perspectives can be a much greater challenge to teachers; there is a tendency to interpret what pupils say in a defensive way.

Action research opens up spaces for such engagement, creating possibilities for growing understanding of young people, and of the activity and purpose of their education, from several different perspectives. We conclude that such collaborative approaches to teacher development are well matched to a broader conception of the role of the teacher at a time when the coordination of services around and including young people is increasingly valued.

Facilitating facilitation: the role of local authorities and children's services

As we have seen, there are significant changes happening in schools in Wales and England, and local authorities and children's services across the UK are also in a state of flux, as we described in Chapter 1. We now revisit these issues to offer suggestions about what can be learned from our findings about how to further develop the role and effectiveness of facilitators such as educational psychologists. Systemic working provides ways of responding to the opportunities presented by the personalisation and interagency agendas, and challenges the traditional methods of interagency working that are typically case-centred.

The story of the project is in one sense the identification of the factors which influence the value of collaborative action research as a process leading to inclusion. The amount of learning entailed in the project suggests that there is a need to make findings available for use by people in other contexts, to encourage and promote effective teacher development in this way. In response to this, the educational psychologists, teachers and university research staff who had been involved in the project collaborated to produce high-quality, accessible, research-informed materials for facilitation of action research for inclusion. These materials have the potential to bring this process to the attention of many potential facilitators and practitioners.

Creating these materials was a powerful collaborative process in itself, maintaining continued academic engagement by those involved in this process. Workshops were held in which practitioners new to the project worked with the materials, giving valuable feedback. No one approach fits all situations, and so the materials describe a range of strategies that can be available to a facilitator to deploy flexibly according to the demands of the situation. The guidelines focus on what can be done:

- Find ways to prepare the ground with senior managers and teachers before beginning the project, including establishing knowledge and setting expectations about action research as a developmental process.
- Define what being a facilitator should and should not be, including different aspects of the role and distinguishing it from leadership.
- Devise important strategies for maintaining momentum, for example, facilitating the right balance between reflection and action, remaining flexible to respond to new and emergent influences on the process.
- Explore how to play a role in creating a wider impact within the secondary school.

The materials do not assume a particular kind of teacher, and neither do they suggest the need for predetermined outcomes to be met. This is congruent with the case studies in terms of the diversity of teachers involved and the range of processes that went on in practice. We are concerned primarily with the creation of a context for this learning, through changes that can take place *within* schools.

However, these are not changes that can be sustained by individual professionals in services; recognition in the service is important. Some EPs felt at least encouraged by their peers and others in the service:

'Just been part of everyday work. PEP very positive and feels EP should have these skills. No special arrangements made to cover my work. PEP encouraging' (EP at Cwrt)

'It's really made me want . . . to facilitate this kind of thing in other schools. And to make it clearer that it's part of our agenda' (EP at Main Road).

Whereas, for other EPs, the feeling was that their involvement was not sustainable without more support from managers:

> 'I've done this as extra work. There's no possibility of cover. No extra payment. Little interest at [LA] management level. Not been invited to feed back' (EP at Parc)

> 'I've had half day locum cover for the whole project. Directed to take rest out of different diary aspects. It has been difficult to juggle competing priorities. Periodic request for feedback from PEP' (EP at Neuadd).

In many cases the LA representative held a perspective which matched that of the EP. For example:

> We don't engage effectively with parents, teachers and children around their needs. We're not yet fundamentally systematic. . . . We need to show heads that systematic EP work is worthwhile' (representative of Neuadd's LA).

As we have seen, there is support from the Welsh Assembly Government for localism in public sector decision-making. This decentralisation can make local services more responsive to local needs, but was perceived by some Welsh LA interviewees as lacking strategic leadership: 'There is a lack of coherent Welsh approach to inclusion. WAG are leaving a lot to local discretion' (Bont/Pentre LA).

Other LA representatives talked about the WAG's emphasis on inclusion being 'right, proper and long overdue' (Tregib LA). The children's services agenda was broadly welcomed in England and Wales, but there was another observation too from Welsh LAs – that the 'tone of UK central government is not inclusive. Publishing league tables makes it harder.' It may be a problem for some local authorities to justify strong or distinctive approaches to inclusion locally which they do not see being pressed forward in the Welsh Assembly, and which is after all invested with Welsh identity and carries considerable expectations. In any case, it was clear that the LAs' influence on schools' approaches to inclusion varied considerably in strength and direction, and only sometimes was there a clear sense of the need to systematically consider teacher development as a critical factor.

There is then a need to look at how local authorities can influence the context in which potential facilitators work, to enhance the possibilities for such work. Spillane (2002) has done some interesting work on the theories of change of district education officers in the United States, in relation to teacher development. His analysis builds on significant ethnographic data and offers a description of three broad perspectives – behaviourist, situated, cognitive – in terms of officers' beliefs about teaching and learning, the curriculum, and motivation. The 'behaviourist' approach is typified by passive reception of knowledge by the learner from an expert: 'Knowledge was treated as a commodity that could be deposited in the minds of teachers through demonstrating and telling' (Spillane 2002, p. 387).

This is in contrast to the 'situated' perspective in which learning is more active and grounded in its socio-cultural context: 'Knowledge is not so much a commodity imported through the words and deeds of experts but constructed in part through reflection and thinking enabled by peers about their practice and guided by the ideas and questions posed by experts' (p. 393). The 'cognitive' approach views learning as the reconstruction, rather than passive assimilation of new knowledge, but does not regard the social context as crucial.

Spillane's findings indicated that the 'behaviourist' approach was most prevalent and adopted by most district officers; a minority follow a 'situated' perspective and only one was in the 'cognitive' category. Indeed, the 'behaviourist' approach accounted for the perspective of 85 per cent of district education officials in their articulation of thinking about teacher change. This was characterised by transmission of information, fragmentation of curriculum and extrinsic motivation. Spillane (2002) tentatively concludes that this emphasis on 'behaviourist' approaches is a product of societal assumptions about the nature of teaching and learning, and also of the fragmented nature of the officials' own work:

> most district change agents had a variety of responsibilities, including grant writing, procuring curricular materials, organizing and carrying out professional development . . . Enabling teacher change and teacher learning was never the sole responsibility of these district change agents.
>
> (Spillane 2002, p. 410)

He goes on to show that the implementation of change is much higher in the minority of districts where the officials adhere to a 'situated' perspective. A school principal working in this way was cited: 'you enable teachers who want to change, putting them in a position where they can do that . . . moving them with a group of people that will go with them . . . it's almost like an art form' (p. 391).

Significantly, Spillane (2002) was able to ascertain that, of these two broad approaches, it was the 'situated' approach which was consistently the most effective in supporting effective and sustainable teacher change. What this indicates is the value of clear leadership in terms of how teacher learning is to be conceived and understood. This is a call for a much more situated understanding of teachers' capacities for professional development of themselves and their practice, and for making opportunities available to facilitate, embed and celebrate this learning, specifically in relation to inclusion.

Conclusion: improving the context for inclusion by personalising teacher learning

Finally we return to what schools and teachers themselves can do to put in place the context of support that is needed to enable teachers to use action research to improve pupils' inclusion. We described in Chapter 2 why this can be challenging, particularly in secondary schools. Building on the findings that we presented in Chapters 5 and 6, we offer here some clear principles and guidelines for teachers and those who support their practice – and we do so in relation to the agenda for personalised learning.

Not all the teachers in the schools that we worked with felt as though they were appreciated and empowered by their senior managers. Some of them felt relatively disillusioned with their position in the school; others felt that they had little understanding of some pupils, and little to offer them. But it was not only one type of teacher who got involved and became central to the success of a project. Some were among those who felt marginalised in the school; others were already recognised as having an influence. Some were experienced; others relatively new entrants to the profession; some saw the project as a way of raising their profile within the school; others were more interested in tackling a stubborn issue in terms of the pupils whom they felt able to reach. What was common to all the teachers who became engaged in these changes was:

•   a sense of enjoyment in working with some of their colleagues on questions of practice, with the opportunity to be creative together;
•   acknowledgement that their relationship with pupils was worth working on;

- relatively little defensiveness about their practice, and openness to the ideas of others when it came to effectively motivating pupils – including the questioning of assumptions by a trusted external facilitator;
- surprise and satisfaction from the sense of achievement that came from spending time addressing issues that were often ignored;
- an ability to link outcomes of the project with (for example) appraisal needs, further professional development processes, and other agendas such as assessment for learning.

In the case studies and the chapters which followed, it became clear that this approach is surprisingly effective at tapping into the talents and abilities of those more experienced teachers who are not aiming for leadership positions; teachers who typically get sidelined, but who greatly influence the educational experience of young people:

> 'There are lots of teachers in schools who've taught for maybe fourteen to fifteen years and don't want to be managers, and who get ignored and sidelined in the community. They'd chosen not to go for promotion, and consequently they are overlooked by those in management. But often they've chosen to stay as practitioners, and so this is an approach which could help them to continue developing their practice, encouraging, supporting, valuing. . . .

> 'This approach is distinctive because unlike NPQH it's about teaching and learning. Not management. All the stuff I do for NPQH in the end is about me as a manager, not a teacher' (Head of History, Main Road).

If we consider what it was about the process which attracted the involvement of this group of teachers in particular, then the ownership that comes with choosing the issue to work on seems very important. Along with this comes the enjoyment of contributing from one's experience, at the same time as learning from others:

> 'Being the senior member in terms of age . . . I keep saying there's only so many trick you can teach an old dog. I think I've found it harder to adjust to the pupil voice element. It must be frustrating for Anne because I don't move along as quickly as she does in terms of taking on board the issues and keeping them going. So I have to remind myself that it is part of the project and I'm due to do this, I'm due to do that, I've got to do that, I've got to do the raffle tickets, so

it's less of an embedded attitude of me. But it has changed my teaching because there is now much more dialogue between the pupils and me and the nature of the work and what I'm doing. We explore the objectives and the reasons for doing what we're doing and what we're not doing in particular so it's something I wouldn't have done much of' (senior teacher, History Department, Main Road).

There is a very close alignment between the features of the process elaborated in this book with the 2020 Vision report on personalising learning, which highlights approaches to continuing professional development that are congruent with making learning more meaningful for pupils:

- *Much of the activity should be school-based, with a sustained focus on improving learning and teaching.* This is not to say that external courses have no place, rather, that such courses are not enough in themselves to effect transfer of knowledge and skills.
- *Much of the activity should be closely integrated with, and run parallel to, the daily or routine practices of teachers, since it is here where change is most difficult but also most needed.* This entails sustained work with teachers in their classrooms.
- *Much of the activity should involve teachers working together in small teams.* This allows teachers to learn from each other and keep each other focused on the task. It also makes individual teachers accountable to their peers for effecting the changes they promise to make, making it more likely that they will do so.
- *Knowledge and skills transfer is usually slow and takes time to perfect and embed.* Everybody would prefer an easy quick fix, but improving learning and teaching is often slow and hard. Making small, incremental changes is more likely to result in sustainable change.
- *Teachers need to be able to choose the practices they change and the techniques they use.* Within areas where change will make a difference (often defined in terms of whole-school priorities), there are often a number of different approaches. Giving teachers the choice about the specific changes they make will mean they are more likely to take responsibility for them, while allowing for collective and consistent strategies to be developed school-wide.
- *Teachers need to see unfamiliar new practices being used in practice.* It is not enough for teachers to read or be told about effective learning and teaching. They need to see it in real classrooms for themselves and be able to question the staff and pupils. One recent

development is schools' 'open days' when staff from other schools
can visit to see the school at work.

(Gilbert 2007, p. 32)

The danger with all lists of this kind is that they become a checklist of
surface features against which to evaluate the character of CPD
opportunities in school, for example. Reading this list in relation to the
process discussed here suggests that it is important to consider ways in
which these features might cohere into an approach to CPD, with
collaborative action research being one way. Some school leaders tend
to work with a relatively mechanistic view of professional development,
which in our experience often overlooks the resources and abilities
that a diverse staff offer. Even so, action research as an approach to
developing inclusion can fit easily into a headteacher's working model,
if there is space in that model to support groups of teachers in taking
the initiative; for example:

Interviewer: So what's really interesting, again from our point of
view, is . . . this is an action research project, we think that
teachers engaging in these types of things and then coming up
with ideas and then really thinking that this is their kind of
thing is a really important part of how a school works, as well
as the kind of structural things you can do like setting up the
House . . . you know, it's about the relationship of those two
things that I think is really interesting.

Head of Main Road: I think as well, in this school, there is culture
of people feeling, being able to run with things.

Interviewer: Yeah. That's really important.

Head of Main Road: We've got a lot of really creative people on
the staff and they get fired up about something. They didn't
think 'I'd love to have been able to do that', they say 'Can I',
you know, 'Is there any chance I could . . .'. So we've got
pockets of good practice in lots of different areas in the school
and there's always something happening. There's always
somebody running something or having an idea and doing it
or . . .

Interviewer: I think that one of the most difficult things must be
though, it kind of comes out in what we've been saying, is that
the difficulty of kind of connecting those things.

Head of Main Road: Yeah, and also not losing the focus on
achievement.

(interview in Main Road)

This headteacher exemplifies the life of a leader who is stretched by a combination of forces pulling in different ways, and yet who has appreciated the need to offer, at a minimum, a benign space in which teachers can act together.

As a way of bringing together these opportunities and qualities, we want to suggest that fundamental to the creation of a context for inclusion is bringing about the **personalisation of teacher development**. This means creating conditions and processes which don't ignore but take seriously the particular contribution of each member of staff in terms of:

- who they are
- what they bring
- what they believe in, struggle with, aim for.

The diagram developed in Chapter 4 (Figure 4.1) can be adapted to emphasise our view of this type of action research as personalised teacher development (Figure 7.1).

In this book we have focused on teachers, but we would be the first to agree that all staff in a school should be considered in this way. Focusing on teachers could be interpreted as encouraging unhelpful distinctions among the increasingly diverse staff who work in secondary schools, but in our view it is a necessary contribution when there is such a strong tendency to exclude teachers from the inclusion debate. A fuller perspective would set this view of teachers within the context of an increasingly rich

Personalised teacher development			Inclusion
Pedagogical actions	**Processes**		Young people's learning and participation
• Teaching approaches • Learning resources • Institutional organisation	• Joint activity (collaboration) • Group interaction with evidence • Discussing, reflecting, focusing, decision-making • Creativity and borrowing of ideas • Contributions of individuals		Teacher learning and participation (re roles, relationships, assumptions)
	emergence		
	Enabling features of context		**Development of context**
	• Group ownership of issue • Diversity of experience • Time • Facilitation of process • Links to other institutional processes		Institutional and interagency development which values and embeds these enabling features

Figure 7.1 Personalising teacher development for inclusion

set of possible relationships in schools. One possibility is to extend the example that this project represents, of multi-agency work which is connected to the schools' core functions and involves teachers alongside many different practitioners. This is a possibility for later.

For whichever staff though, personalisation is not about listening to them and paying attention to their perspectives *for the sake of it*. The case studies have also clearly shown the importance of the issues teachers actively contribute to, which include significant themes in the psychology and sociology of learning – motivation, the role of assessment, prejudice about social class. Personalising teacher development results, we believe, in unlocking more of the potential that teachers have to create meaningful education for young people.

Teachers do have choices. Our findings show that when teachers recognise the choices they have, and the fact that they can make a difference to their pupils' experience and participation in school, a stepchange can take place in their level of satisfaction and fulfilment in the job. Taking a longer perspective, one of the most frustrating aspects of such work is when it runs out of steam and appears to lead to no sustained changes in the institution. But teachers can influence colleagues, and with appropriate facilitation they can create opportunities for others in the school to consider what has been identified or developed, and whether and how it might be applied in their own particular context. This involves teachers in talking about their work with others in the school, and indeed in other schools, in a credible, practical and dialogic manner, and then making themselves available – by linking into other ongoing agendas and structures – to assist in related developments with other staff. It is common in schools to deal with projects, processes and structures as if they are separate from each other, in a way which amplifies that sense of separateness. We urge teachers not to make so many distinctions, and to see themselves as one of a team of multi-skilled, adaptable and collaborative professionals which is based in school but which extends beyond it.

Conclusion

Inclusion is not a quick fix. It involves a change in culture, and this can sound utopian, but it has a pragmatic impact. An investment is needed – time, resources, priorities – and there are plenty of reasons

continued

to question the wisdom of this investment. But in this book we have argued that:

1   There is a clear justification for this investment in inclusion. Inclusion is the main mission of schools as educational institutions.

2   There is a practical and efficient way forward: shift understandings of teaching, build on the expectation that teachers are critically reflective about their practice, and make it possible for teachers working collaboratively to investigate, expand their understandings and become more openly enquiring about the experience and engagement of the young people they work with. In other words, treat teachers as people, and personalise teacher development.

3   There are resources available locally to support this process in schools. There is no assumption here that groups of teachers should or can challenge their own assumptions on their own, or reinvent the wheel in terms of improvements to their practice. Facilitation by other professionals and engaging with young people in different ways can promote a wider discourse about young people and how teachers can and should relate to them, and can offer access to relevant and timely resources.

Inclusion is a serious proposition for an education system which cares about the impact that it has on the lives of the young people who experience it. Facilitating the conditions for inclusion constitutes a considerable challenge in terms of educational policy at all levels, as we have shown. But in our experience, engaging with the issue of inclusion can be enjoyable and intrinsically rewarding for teachers, sustain their professionalism, and make a positive difference to those young people.

How was the research carried out?

Prosiect Dysgu Cydradd was a collaborative development and research project involving Trinity College Carmarthen and the University of Manchester, six local authorities and seven secondary schools in those authorities. The aim was to learn more about the factors that influence teacher engagement in structured reflective practice towards more inclusive learning for pupils, and how such practice could be supported in schools. Prosiect Dysgu Cydradd took place in two successive phases (June 2005 to March 2006 and June 2006 to March 2007).

Research questions

1   What factors relating to teachers and their learning environment facilitate or hinder schools/teachers from engaging in collaborative action research with the aim of developing inclusion?
2   What features of practice, organisation or external support can enhance these facilitating factors, or mitigate hindering ones?
3   What evidence is there of a relationship between teacher engagement in collaborative action research towards more inclusive practice and the learning and participation of pupils?
4   In respect of these questions, what are the significant differences between the Welsh and English contexts?

Personnel and research sites

Two lead researchers coordinated the research process, negotiating and agreeing a systematic approach to the intervention and data generation between the two university groups. We created and maintained communication structures among participants in the project, dealt with issues arising in schools and LEAs in relation to the development and research process, and participated in and managed the generation and interpretation of data. Research assistants with experience in UK schools supported the generation of data within the action research projects, and generated data on the engagement of teachers, the facilitation by EPs, and on pupil participation and engagement, through observations in schools and by conducting interviews and focus groups with teachers, EPs and pupils.

Six schools, each from different local authorities, were selected to provide a range of size and geographical location, institutional experience with action research, and national policy contexts. One school withdrew from the project halfway through, and was replaced with another in the same local authority. Four of the schools were in Wales, and two of these were Welsh medium schools. The other two schools were in England.

The development and research process

Each school was invited to identify a group of staff to participate in a school project. In most cases this was an existing group of teachers, often a subject department, who then agreed and worked on an action research project with the aim of developing their educational inclusion. To contextualise and clarify the potentially nebulous concept of inclusion in the experience of teachers and learners, these groups were invited to reflect on pupil engagement with learning, to identify an issue facing them relating to this concept, and to make that the focus of their action research. This pattern was repeated with a different group of teachers from the same school in the following year: following analysis of the findings from Phase 1, new ways of working were explored in Phase 2. **Data about the school context** were generated through local authority and headteacher interviews at the start of the project and headteacher interviews at the end. Teachers and EPs gave opinions and feedback about school-level factors by their responses to questionnaire items and verbal feedback given during network days and on researchers' visits to school. On visits to project schools, researchers made ad hoc classroom observations, engaged in discussions in staffrooms, and observed interactions between staff and pupils, providing an opportunity to observe how teacher projects were developing in the schools.

Throughout the process, the school's educational psychologist (EP) was asked to act as a facilitator and critical friend to the teacher group. These EPs became part of the **core development and research group** which met every six months for a day, usually held in Newtown, Powys (halfway between Carmarthen and Manchester). In these sessions and in three-monthly follow-up meetings at the two universities, materials and training were offered to the EPs to prepare them for the facilitation role, and EPs provided feedback and insights into the processes underway in their schools. The processes that developed in schools, and the factors that constrained and assisted teacher involvement were monitored and studied by the EP and researchers. In order to further refine understanding of these factors, to learn about how to sustain changes in practice and about how to influence the wider school, the whole process was repeated in the schools during the following year with a different group of staff. **Data about the views of EPs** were generated during regular project meetings, and supplemented with interviews where appropriate. An EP questionnaire after each phase invited them to comment on the factors that had impacted on the teacher project, the teachers' engagement and their own involvement. These data provided information about school factors at teacher and EP level that affected teacher engagement.

The purpose of the data that were gathered was to identify the issues and challenges that had hindered progress, and the factors that had facilitated teacher engagement with their projects. Teachers' initial knowledge and opinions of inclusion and action research were assessed prior to any school project meetings using two project questionnaires to identify any significant influences on subsequent engagement. Teacher perspectives were also gauged during teacher focus groups, facilitated by the EP. These provided a starting point for teachers to explore ambiguities and untested assumptions in their thinking on the issue they were working on. Formal interviews and informal discussions were conducted with teachers when researchers visited schools, and on the four networking days involving teachers from the different schools. Video conferencing on these days facilitated contact between Welsh and English groups. At the end of their project a sample of teachers were interviewed and all teachers were invited to complete a questionnaire which asked them to reflect on the factors that had helped and hindered the approach, the impact on them and their pupils, and how it compared with other methods of continuing professional development. Seeking teacher perspectives through their projects provided a rich source of data about their engagement, and what affected it.

To identify any relationship between changes in pupil responses and teacher engagement, three questionnaires were administered to relevant pupils before and after the teacher projects. In the absence of any directly relevant published instrument to test pupils' assessment of inclusivity of lessons, two related published questionnaires were adopted: the Myself As Learner Scale (Burden 1998) and the Individual Classroom Environment Questionnaire (Rentoul and Fraser 1979), both published in Frederickson and Cameron (1999), and a further questionnaire was designed and trialled in the project ('What I think about school' – see below). In addition, pupil focus groups were held with a cross-section of pupils who had completed the questionnaires, in which researchers encouraged pupils to consider the impact of teacher projects and their general perspectives on inclusion. These were analysed using descriptive and inferential statistics.

Teachers evaluated the impact of their projects on pupils in a third teacher questionnaire and during follow-up interviews.

Trustworthiness

Research which involves direct engagement in activity by participants gains an inherent advantage in respect of trustworthiness. Actions speak louder than words, and the actions and activities of teachers and educational psychologists were an important source of evidence about the relevance of the approaches being facilitated in the school projects. The range of data on participant perspectives described above was used to triangulate this action-oriented data, revealing some of the congruence, contradiction and difference which characterise any real life process.

Emerging interpretations of the nature and impact of the processes underway in schools were regularly tested with EPs and teachers in project meetings, and as the project developed further, in the context of workshop and research conference presentations in which EPs, teachers and university researchers were involved.

Pupil questionnaire: What I think about school

We are trying to find out what you think about your lessons, so that teachers can take this into account in their planning.

Name _____   Year ____   Boy/Girl ____

What lesson have you just had? _____ To answer the following questions, think about the lessons you have had this term in this subject. Tick the box that best fits what you think. There are no right or wrong answers to these questions. Please give the completed questionnaire back to your teacher.

Table A1 Pupil questionnaire: What I think about school

	Always	Usually	Not usually	Never
1 The teacher knows everyone in the class				
2 The teacher cares about how I get on				
3 The teacher tells me when I do well				
4 The teacher helps me out when I get stuck				
5 The teacher encourages us to ask questions				
6 My ideas are listened to and used in discussions				
7 I feel involved in classroom activities				
8 I like working in small groups in this class				
9 The teacher tells me off if I don't do the work				
10 I like having challenging work to do				
11 I feel anxious or upset when I get stuck				
12 We get easy work to do in these lessons				
13 I enjoy answering the teacher's questions				
14 I enjoy this lesson				
15 The work we get given is boring				
16 We can choose the work we do				
17 I give my opinion during discussions				
18 I learn new things in this lesson				
19 Pupils help each other on difficult problems				
20 We do a lot of work from textbooks				
21 The lesson is really interesting for me				
22 The teacher uses words that I don't understand				
23 We do lots of different activities in the lesson				
24 I understand what the teacher wants us to do				

References

Ainscow, M., T. Booth, A. Dyson, A. Howes, F. Gallannaugh, R. Smith, P. Farrell and J. Frankham (2006). *Improving Schools, Developing Inclusion*. London, Routledge.

Allan, J. (2003). 'Productive pedagogies and the challenge of inclusion.' *British Journal of Special Education* **30**(4): 175–179.

Avramidis, E., P. D. Bayliss and R. L. Burden (2002). 'Inclusion in action: an in-depth case study of an effective inclusive secondary school in the south-west of England.' *International Journal of Inclusive Education* **6**(2): 143.

Ball, S. J. (1997). 'Policy sociology and critical social research: a personal review of recent education policy and policy research.' *British Educational Research Journal* **23**(3): 257.

Benjamin, S., M. Nind, K. Hall, J. Collins and K. Sheehy (2003). 'Moments of inclusion and exclusion: pupils negotiating classroom contexts.' *British Journal of Sociology of Education* **24**(5): 547–558.

Bentley, T., D. Hopkins *et al.* (2005). Developing a network perspective. In *What Are We Learning About . . . ? Establishing a Network of Schools*. Nottingham, NCSL.

Bernstein, B. (1996). *Pedagogy, Symbolic Control and Identity*. London, Taylor & Francis.

Blatchford, P., E. Baines, C. Rubie-Davies, P. Bassett and A. Chowne (2006). 'The effect of a new approach to group work on pupil–pupil and teacher–pupil interactions.' *Journal of Educational Psychology* **98**(4): 750–765.

Booth, T. and M. Ainscow (eds) (1998). *From Them to Us: An International Study of Inclusion in Education*. London, Routledge.

Booth, T., M. Ainscow, K. Black-Hawkind, M. Vaughan and L. Shaw (2000). *Index for Inclusion: Developing Learning and Participation in Schools*. Bristol, Centre for Studies on Inclusive Education.

Boyle, B. and J. Bragg (2006). 'A curriculum without foundation.' *British Educational Research Journal* **32**(4): 569–582.

Bronfenbrenner, U. (1979). *The Ecology of Human Development: Experiments by Nature and Design*. Cambridge, MA, Harvard University Press.

Burden, R. L. (1998). 'Assessing children's perceptions of themselves as learners and problem solvers.' *School Psychology International* **19**(4): 291–305.

Calder, G. (2003). Communitarianism and New Labour. http://www.whb.co.uk/socialissues/vol2gc.htm.

Carrington, S. and J. Elkins (2002). 'Bridging the gap between inclusive policy and inclusive culture in secondary schools.' *Support for Learning* **17**(2): 51–57.

Centre for Equity in Education (CEE) (2008). *Equity in Education: Responding to Context.* The third report on the state of equity in the English education system. Centre for Equity in Education, The University of Manchester.

Clark, C., A. Dyson, and A. Millward (1999). 'Theories of inclusion, theories of schools: deconstructing and reconstructing the "inclusive school".' *British Educational Research Journal* **25**(2): 157–177.

Clough, P. (2000). Routes to inclusion. In P. Clough and J. Corbett, *Theories of Inclusive Education.* London, Sage.

Cochran-Smith, M. and S. Lytle (1999). 'Relationships of knowledge and practice: teacher learning in communities.' *Review of Research in Education* **24**: 249–305.

Colley, H. (2007). 'Unbecoming teachers: towards a more dynamic notion of professional participation.' *Journal of Education Policy* **22**(2): 173.

Connell, J. P. and A. C. Kubisch (1998). Applying a theories of change approach to the design and evaluation of comprehensive community initiatives: progress, prospects, and problems. In K. Fulbright-Anderson, A. C. Kubisch and J. P. Connell, *New Approaches to Evaluating Community Initiatives: Theory, Measurement, and Analysis.* Washington, DC, The Aspen Institute (Vol. II).

Corbett, J. and B. Norwich (1999). Common or specialised pedagogy? In P. Mortimer, *Understanding Pedagogy and its Impact on Learning.* London, Paul Chapman.

Cordingley, P., M. Bell, B. Rundell and D. Evans (2003). The impact of collaborative CPD on classroom teaching and learning: how does collaborative continuing professional development (CPD) for teachers of the 5–16 age range affect teaching and learning? *Research Evidence in Education Library.* London, EPPI-Centre, Social Science Research Unit, Institute of Education, University of London.

Cummings, C., A. Dyson, D. Muijs, I. Papps, D. Pearson, C. Raffo, L. Tiplady and L. Todd (2007). *Evaluation of the Full Service Extended Schools Initiative: Final Report Brief No: RB852.* London, DCSF.

Daugherty, R. and S. M. B. Davies (2008). *Capacity and Quality in Education Research in Wales.* A stimulus report for the Strategic Forum for Research in Education. Harrogate.

Daugherty, R. and G. E. Jones (2002). 'The learning country.' *Welsh Journal of Education* **11**: 107–113.

Davidson, J. (2001). *Wales: The Learning Country.* Cardiff, Welsh Assembly Government.

Davies, S. M. B. and A. Howes (2006). *'I haven't got time to think!': Contradictions as Drivers for Change in an Analysis of Joint Working Between Teachers and School Psychologists*. Twenty-eighth International School Psychology Colloquium, Hangzhou, China, 15 to 20 July.

Davies, S. M. B., A. Howes, S. Fox, P. Farrell, G. Squires and M. Hancock (in press). *Personalising Teacher Development: Collaborative Action Research to Change Schools*.

DCSF (2008). *Social and Emotional Aspects of Learning (SEAL)*: Curriculum resource introductory booklet. London, HMSO.

Department of Health and The Home Office (2003). *The Victoria Climbié Inquiry, Report of an Inquiry by Lord Laming*. **CM 5730**.

DES (1978). *Special Educational Needs (Warnock Report)*. London, HMSO.

DfEE (2000). *Educational Psychology Services (England): Current Role, Good Practice and Future Directions. Report on the DfEE Working Group on the Role and training of Educational Psychologists*. London, HMSO.

DFES (2002). *SEN Code of Practice (Revised Version)*. London, HMSO.

Earl, L. M. (2003). *Assessment as Learning: Using Classroom Assessment to Maximize Student Learning*, Thousand Oaks, CA, Corwin Press.

Elliott, J. (1991). *Action Research for Educational Change*. Buckingham, Open University Press.

Elliott, J. (2007). 'Assessing the quality of action research.' *Research Papers in Education* **22**(2): 229–246.

Englebrecht, P. (2004). 'Changing roles for educational psychologists within inclusive education in South Africa.' *School Psychology International* **25**(1): 20–29.

Eraut, M. (2005). *Typologies for Investigating What is Learned in the Workplace and How?* European Association for Research on Learning and Instruction (EARLI Conference), Nicosia.

Farrell, P. (2004). 'Making inclusion a reality for all.' *School Psychology International* **25**(1): 5–19.

Farrell, P., S. R. Jimerson, A. Kalambouka and J. Beniot (2005). 'Teachers' perceptions of school psychologists in different countries.' *School Psychology International* **26**(5): 525–544.

Farrell, P., K. Woods, S. Lewis, S. Rooney, G. Squires and M. O'Connor (2006). *A Review of Educational Psychologists in England and Wales in Light of 'Every Child Matters: Change for Children'*. London, Department for Education and Skills.

Fielding, M. (2006). 'Leadership, personalization and high performance schooling: naming the new totalitarianism.' *School Leadership & Management* **26**(4): 347–369.

Fielding, M. and S. Bragg (2003). *Students as Researchers; Making a Difference*. Cambridge, Pearson.

Fish, S. (1994). *There's No Such Thing as Free Speech*. Oxford, Oxford University Press.

Florian, L. and M. Rouse (2001). 'Inclusive practice in English secondary schools: lessons learned.' *Cambridge Journal of Education* **31**(3): 399–412.

Franke, M. L., T. P. Carpenter *et al.* (1998). *Teachers as Learners: Developing Understanding Through Children's Thinking*. Paper presented at the annual meeting of the American Educational Research Association, San Diego, CA.

Frankham, J. (2006). 'Network utopias and alternative entanglements for educational research and practice.' *Journal of Education Policy* **21**(6): 661–677.

Frankham, J. and A. Howes (2006). 'Talk as action in "collaborative action research": making and taking apart teacher/researcher relationships.' *British Educational Research Journal* **32**(4): 617–632.

Frederickson, N. and R. J. Cameron (1999). *Psychology in Education Portfolio*. Chiswick, NFER-Nelson.

Fuller, A., H. Hodkinson, P. Hodkinson and L. Unwin (2005). 'Learning as peripheral participation in communities of practice: a reassessment of key concepts in workplace learning.' *British Educational Research Journal* **31**(1): 49–68.

Furlong, J. (2000). Intuition and the crisis in teacher professionalism. In T. Atkinson and G. Claxton, *The Intuitive Practitioner, On the Value of Not Always Knowing What One is Doing*. Buckingham, Open University Press.

Gilbert, C. (2007). *2020 Vision: Report of the Teaching and Learning in 2020 Review Group*. London, DfES.

Gilligan, C. (1982). *In a Different Voice: Psychological Theory and Women's Development*. Cambridge, MA, Harvard University Press.

González, N., L. C. Moll and C. Amanti (2005). *Funds of Knowledge: Theorizing Practices in Households, Communities, and Classrooms*, Engelwoods Cliffs, NJ, Lawrence Erlbaum.

Goodson, I. (2003). *Professional Knowledge, Professional Lives: Studies in Education and Change (Professional Learning)*. Buckingham, Open University Press.

Grace, G. (1994). Urban education and the culture of contentment: the politics, culture and economics of inner-city schooling. In N. P. Stromquist, *Education in Urban Areas. Cross-national Dimensions*. Westport, CT, Praeger.

Haggarty, L. and K. Postlethwaite (2003). 'Action research: a strategy for teacher change and school development?' *Oxford Review of Education* **29**(4): 423–448.

Hargreaves, A. (1997). From reform to renewal: a new deal for a new age. In A. Hargreaves and R. Evans, *Beyond Educational Reform. Bringing Teachers Back In*. Buckingham, Open University Press.

Hayden, M. and J. Thompson (2007). 'Policy-making in practice: issues arising from evaluation of the Welsh Baccalaureate.' *Welsh Journal of Education* **14**(1): 85–99.

Hextall, I., S. Gewirtz, A. Cribb and P. Mahoney (2007). *Changing Teacher Roles, Identities and Professionalism: An Annotated Bibliography*. London, Kings College and Roehampton University.

HMSO (1968). *Psychologists in Education Services (Summerfield Report)*. London, HMSO.

Hoban, G. J. (2002). *Teacher Learning for Educational Change (Professional Learning)*. London, Open University Press.

Hopkins, D. (2007). *Every School a Great School: Realizing the Potential of System Leadership*. Maidenhead, Open University Press.

Howes, A. and S. Fox (2006). *Understanding Action Research with Professionals in Schools: Accounting for Legitimate and Persistent Discourses as Part of the Real-world Experience of Changing Practice*. British Educational Research Association Conference, Warwick, 6 to 9 September.

Hustler, D., O. McNamara, J. Jarvis, M. Londra, A. Campbell and J. Howson (2003). 'Teachers' perceptions of continuing professional development.' *DfES Research Report RR*. **429**.

Kemmis, S. (2001). Exploring the relevance of critical theory for action research: emancipatory action research in the footsteps of Jurgen Habermas. In P. Reason and H. Bradbury, *Handbook of Action Research: participative inquiry and practice*. London, Sage.

Knight, P. (2002). 'A systemic approach to professional development: learning as practice.' *Teaching and Teacher Education* **18**(3): 229–241.

Kugelmass, J. (2004). *The Inclusive School: Sustaining Equity and Standards*. New York, Teachers College Press.

Kwakman, K. (2003). 'Factors affecting teachers' participation in professional learning activities.' *Teaching and Teacher Education* **19**(2): 149–170.

Lave, J. and E. Wenger (1991). *Situated Learning: Legitimate Peripheral Participation*. Cambridge, Cambridge University Press.

Lord, P., K. Kinder, A. Wilkin, M. Atkinson and J. Harland (2008). *Evaluating the Early Impact of Integrated Children's Services: Round 1 Summary Report*. Slough, NFER.

Louis, K. S., H. M. Marks and S. Kruse (1996). 'Teachers' professional community in restructuring schools.' *American Educational Research Journal* **33**(4): 757–798.

Lupton, R. (2006). How does place affect education? In S. Delorenzi, *Going Places: Neighbourhood, Ethnicity and Social Mobility*. London, Institute of Public Policy Research.

MacIntyre, A. (1984). *After Virtue: A Study in Moral Theory*. NotreDame, University of Notre Dame Press.

McLaughlin, T. H. (2003). 'Teaching as a practice and a community of practice: the limits of commonality and the demands of diversity.' *Journal of Philosophy of Education* **37**(2): 339–352.

Mahony, P. and I. Hextall (2000). *Reconstructing Teaching: Standards, Performance and Accountability*. London, Routledge.

Moon, J. (1999). *Reflection in Learning & Professional Development: Theory & Practice*. London, Routledge.

Morrison, K. (1996). 'Developing reflective practice in higher degree students through a learning journal.' *Studies in Higher Education* **21**(3): 317–332.

Moss, G. (2004). 'Changing practice: the National Literacy Strategy and the politics of literacy policy.' *Literacy* **38**(3): 126–133.

Muijs, D. and G. Lindsay (2008). 'Where are we at? An empirical study of levels and methods of evaluating continuing professional development.' *British Educational Research Journal* **34**(2): 195–211.

NAfW (2001). *The Learning Country: A Paving Document: A Comprehensive Education and Lifelong Learning Programme to 2010 in Wales*. Cardiff, National Assembly for Wales.

NAfW (2002). *Special Educational Needs Code of Practice for Wales*. Cardiff, National Assembly for Wales.

NAfW (2004a). *Educational Psychology in Wales*. Cardiff, National Assembly for Wales.

NAfW (2004b). *Learning Pathways Through Statutory Assessment: Key Stages 2 and 3: Daugherty Assessment Review Group Final Report*. Cardiff, Welsh Assembly Government.

National College for School Leadership (NCSL) (2004). *Like No Other Initiative*. Cranfield, NCSL.

Newman, J. (2002). 'Changing governance, changing equality? New Labour, modernisation and pubic services.' *Public Money and Management* **January–March**: 7–13.

Noddings, N. (2001). 'Care and coercion in school reform.' *Journal of Educational Change* **2**(1): 35–43.

Noddings, N. (2003). 'Is teaching a practice?' *Journal of Philosophy of Education* **37**(2): 241.

Norwich, B. (2005). 'Future directions for professional educational psychology.' *School Psychology International* **26**(4): 387–397.

O'Neill, O. (2002). *A Question of Trust: The BBC Reith Lectures 2002*. Cambridge, Cambridge University Press.

Orland-Barak, L. (2006). 'Convergent, divergent and parallel dialogues: knowledge construction in professional conversations.' *Teachers and Teaching* **12**(1): 13–31.

Orland-Barak, L. and H. Tillema (2006). 'The "dark side of the moon": a critical look at teacher knowledge construction in collaborative settings.' *Teachers and Teaching* **12**(1): 1–12.

Osborn, M. (2006). 'Changing the context of teachers' work and professional development: A European perspective.' *International Journal of Educational Research* **45**(4–5): 242–253.

Painter, C. and E. Clarence (2000). 'New Labour and inter-governmental management: flexible networks or performance control?' *Public Management* **2**(4): 477–498.

Pearson, D., A. Dyson, D. Muijs, C. Cummings, L. Tiplady, L. Todd, I. Papps, C. Raffo and D. Crowther (2007). *Evaluation of the Full Service Extended Schools Initiative: Final Report*. Nottingham, DfES.

Raffo, C., A. Dyson, H. Gunter, D. Hall, L. Jones and A. Kalambouka (2007). *Education and Poverty: A Critical Review of Theory, Policy and Practice*. York, Joseph Rowntree Foundation.

Reason, P. and H. Bradbury (eds) (2001). *Handbook of Action Research*. London, Sage.

Rees, G. (2007). 'The impacts of parliamentary devolution on education policy in Wales.' *Welsh Journal of Education* **14**: 8–20.

Rentoul, A. J. and B. J. Fraser (1979). 'Conceptualisation of enquiry based or open classroom environments.' *Journal of Curriculum Studies* **11**: 233–245.

Roaf, C. and H. Bines (1989). Needs, rights and opportunities in special education. In C. Roaf and H. Bines, *Needs, Rights and Opportunities: Developing Approaches in Special Education*. London, Falmer.

Rudduck, J. and J. Flutter (2004). *How to Improve Your School: Giving Pupils a Voice*. London, Continuum.

Russell, B. (1918). *Proposed Roads To Freedom: Socialism, Anarchism and Syndicalism*. New York, Cornwall Press.

Sachs, J. (2000). Rethinking the practice of teacher professionalism. In C. Day, A. Fernandez, T. Hauge and J. Moller, *The Life and Work of Teachers*. London, Falmer Press.

Schon, D. (1983). *The Reflective Practitioner*. London, Teachers College Press.

Shulman, L. S. (1987). 'Knowledge and teaching: foundations of the new reform.' *Harvard Educational Review* **57**(1–2).

Siraj-Blatchford, I., E. Milton, K. Sylva, J. Laugharne and F. Charles (2007). 'Developing the Foundation Phase for 3–7-year-olds in Wales.' *Welsh Journal of Education* **14**(1): 43–68.

Siskin, L. S. and J. W. Little (1995). The subject department: continuities and critiques. In *The Subjects in Question: Departmental Organization and the High School*. New York, Teachers College Press.

Skrtic, T. M. (1991). *Behind Special Education: A Critical Analysis of Professional Culture and School Organization*. New York, Love Publishing Company.

Smylie, M. A. (1995). Teacher learning in the workplace: implications for school reform. In R. Guskey and M. Huberman, *Professional Development in Education: New Paradigms and Practices*. New York, Teachers College Press.

Spillane, J. P. (2002). 'Local theories of teacher change: the pedagogy of district policies and programs.' *The Teachers College Record* **104**(3): 377–420.

Stenhouse, L. (1975). *An Introduction to Curriculum Research and Development*. London, Heinemann.

Stetsenko, A. (2005). 'Activity as object-related: resolving the dichotomy of individual and collective planes of activity.' *Mind, Culture and Activity* 12(1): 70–88.

Sturman, L. (2005). *Professional Life: Teachers' Views in 2004 and 2005*. Paper presented to the British Educational Research Association Annual Conference, University of Glamorgan.

Thomas, G. and G. Glenny (2002). 'Thinking about inclusion: whose reason? whose evidence?' *International Journal of Inclusive Education* 6(4): 345–369.

Thomas, G. and A. Loxley (2001). *Deconstructing Special Education and Constructing Inclusion*. Buckingham, Open University Press.

Thomas, G. and A. Loxley (2007). *Deconstructing Special Education and Constructing Inclusion*. Maidenhead, Open University Press.

Thomson, P. and H. Gunter (2006). 'From "consulting pupils" to "pupils as researchers": a situated case narrative.' *British Educational Research Journal* 32(6): 839–856.

Thrupp, M. (2006). *School Improvement: An Unofficial Approach (Improving Schools)*. London, Continuum.

Thrupp, M. and S. Tomlinson (2005). 'Introduction: education policy, social justice and "complex hope".' *British Educational Research Journal* 31(5): 549–556.

Toole, J. C. and K. S. Louis (2002). 'The role of professional learning communities in international education.' *Second International Handbook of Educational Leadership and Administration* 245–279.

Training and Development Agency for Schools (TDA) (2007). *Guidance to Accompany the Standards for Qualified Teacher Status (QTS)*. London, TDA.

UNESCO (2001). *Open File on Inclusive Education. Support Materials for Managers and Administrators*. Paris, UNESCO.

Vandenberghe, R. (2002). 'Teachers' professional development as the core of school improvement.' *International Journal of Educational Research* 37(8): 653–659.

Watkins, C. (2000). 'Introduction to the articles on consultation.' *Educational Psychology in Practice* 16(1): 5–8.

Welsh Assembly Government (2004). *Educational Psychology in Wales*. Cardiff, Welsh Assembly Government.

Welsh Assembly Government (2005). *Learning Pathways 14–19*. Cardiff, The Department for Education, Lifelong Learning and Skills.

Welsh Assembly Government (2006). *The Learning Country: Vision into Action*. Cardiff, The Department for Education, Lifelong Learning and Skills.

Zollers, N., A. K. Ramanathan and M. Yu (1999). 'The relationship between school culture and inclusion: how an inclusive culture supports inclusive education.' *International Journal of Qualitative Studies in Education* 12(2): 157–174.

Index